ASK YOUR UNCLE
BASEBALL TRIVIA

ASK YOUR UNCLE

BASEBALL TRIVIA

FRANK MORRIS

A Mountain Lion Book

Library of Congress Control Number: 2011944910
ISBN 978-0-9839689-1-7

Cover and text design by Bob Antler, Antler Designworks

Printed in the United States of America

Every effort has been made to make Ask Your Uncle Baseball Trivia as accurate
as possible. Should you have any comments or questions, and/or wish to inform
us of an error, please write or email as follows:

- Frank Morris, 9 Rowell Street, Amesbury, MA 01913
- or fcmorris@gmail.com

CONTENTS

Acknowledgements

I wish to thank good friends who have always shared an appreciation for baseball and its history: Mary Ellen and Julie Morris, Mike Morris, Nate Cahoon, Jim Hayes, Trevor O'Driscoll, John Monteleone, Tom Doherty and Bakey's on Broad and Water. Along with family, this book was made for you guys.

Thank you also to Peter Kollmann, a five-tool editor who contributed yeoman's work editing Uncle's prose, punctuating his sentences, checking his facts, confirming his statistics, and proofing final pages—in other words, expertly making every ball-strike, fair-foul call on the way from manuscript to printed book.

Lastly, thank you Pedro Guerrero and Dwight Evans—forever childhood heroes.

Frank Morris
Spring 2012

Introduction

Ask Your Uncle (AYU) Baseball Trivia is a new standard of trivia. It transcends the mundane, the routine, the journeyman questions and probes far and wide to see just how much you know about the Grand Old Game. Diverse subject categories test your knowledge of:

- players and managers
- lineups of dynasty and championship teams
- career, season and seminal game statistics
- anagrams of baseball hall of fame players
- legendary players' uniform numbers
- great lefty/righty pitcher duos (i.e. Sandy Koufax-Don Drysdale)
- dubious feats (What pitcher has lost the most postseason games?)
- and awarded achievements of yesteryear and yesterday.

In today's sports obsessed culture where a passing cab updates you on the latest baseball scores and statistics—even if you're not a rabid sports fan—the ubiquity of sports information bedazzles everyone with a familiarity, if not appreciation, of the athletes who play our games and claim our championships. On the pages of *AYU Baseball Trivia* you get to test your knowledge of baseball's events and participants—primarily those of the past—to determine what baseball bits from among all of the sports data and information whirling inside your head you can accurately recall. Last man standing wins the AYU Baseball Trivia Cup!

Warning . . . the questions of *AYU Baseball Trivia* are not "cookies" (batting practice-speed fastballs right down the middle of the plate). Rather, *AYU Baseball Trivia* is the stuff of Cooperstown—hall-of-fame quality questions that consistently paint the black. To meet this challenge with knock-it-out-of-the-park answers you will have to bring your best stuff. For example, mainstream minor-league level trivia asks if you can name Most Valuable Players by league, by year, by team, or by position. *AYU Baseball Trivia* asks you to name what Most Valuable Players have brothers talented enough also to play in the major leagues by the clues involving their lesser-accomplished siblings. And we're just warming up!

AYU Baseball Trivia easy-to-use format supplies answers on the next non-facing pages that follow the questions. Readers avoid the annoying rifling through the back of the book trying to match questions to answers. Result: More time examining questions, less time spent shuffling pages. The treatment is not a front-to-back read—open the book randomly while quizzing family, friends or yourself, on the fly, at the bar and lounge or in the Barcalounger.

Any baseball fan that loves the game will categorically enjoy *AYU Baseball Trivia*. And if—by law of averages— there's an answer that scoots by you, ask your uncle. He probably has the answer.

ASK YOUR UNCLE
BASEBALL TRIVIA

MVPS WITH BIG LEAGUE BROTHERS

Not surprisingly, some of baseball's best skilled players had brothers talented enough to play in the majors. Identify these former Most Valuable Players by the clues involving their lesser-known siblings.

1. Brother Billy and this two-time MVP formed a double play combo for six years. Their father kept his boys in check as their manager for one full season in 1987.

2. This 1971 MVP and four-time World Series winning manager grew up in Brooklyn revering older brother Frank, nine years his elder and first baseman for the World Champion Milwaukee Braves.

3. Playing part of three seasons at 6 foot 2 and 220 pounds, brother Ozzie was still outsized by this 1988 MVP twin.

4. For one season in 1972, this recalcitrant White Sox star had two brothers – Ron and Hank – playing in the major leagues. Perhaps having family close by helped him win that year's AL MVP.

5. Bay Area born legend grew up one of nine siblings. Two of them also became MLB All-Stars. Name the three-time MVP, and, if you can, his brothers.

6. He was 1957 MVP for bringing championship to Milwaukee. His younger brother later joined him for seven seasons in Milwaukee and Atlanta.

7. Brother Stephen met his brother, 1995's NL MVP, for a quick coffee in Cincinnati during the 1998 season.

8. Wilton was a highly touted Dodgers prospect whose talent was much as unrealized as his younger brother's was unreal. By the end of their short stint together in Montreal, Wilton's career had all but wilted while his brother's credentials would win him liberation from Canada, a windfall of free-agent cash and the 2004 AL MVP.

9. With brother and Cardinal teammate Walker catching his All-Star start in 1942, the pair formed the only sibling battery in ASG history. Rudy York and Lou Boudreau homers handed him the loss in a 3-1 AL win, but he won when it counted that year – a World Series title and NL MVP Award for his 22-7 record and 1.78 ERA.

10. Well before his brother reached the bigs, older sibling Larry was a
    September call-up on the Astros bullpen staff in 1971. At the threshold of
    his first major league appearance, he injured himself warming up to start
    the ninth and never threw a pitch. Penciled in as replacement to pinch
    hitter Rich Chiles, Larry's name would never be written on another
    scorecard – but it was enough documentation to put him on the books for a
    single game appearance. While no player record has fewer digits, his
    younger brother's twenty-year career with the Brewers accounts for one of
    the most abundant stat totals in MLB history: including more than 3,000
    hits, 11,000 at-bats and two AL MVPs in 1982 and 1989.

MVPS WITH BIG LEAGUE BROTHERS (ANSWERS)

1. Cal Ripken

2. Joe Torre

3. Jose Canseco

4. Richie Allen

5. Joe DiMaggio

6. Hank Aaron

7. Barry Larkin

8. Vladimir Guerrero

9. Mort Cooper

10. Robin Yount

HANK AARON ★★★ Played 1954–1976

Henry Louis "Hammerin' Hank" Aaron crushed 755 home runs. For twenty consecutive years, he compiled 20 home runs per season. Eight times Aaron hit 40 home runs or more. He is the all-time runs-batted-in (RBI) leader, with 2,297 and ranks third in hits, with 3,771. His lifetime batting average was .305. Aaron was inducted into the Baseball Hall of Fame in 1982.

CAREER STATISTICS

Batting average	.305
At bats	12,364
Hits	3,771
Doubles	624
Home runs	755
Runs scored	2,174
Runs batted in	2,297
Bases on balls	1,402

Hank Aaron was born on February 5, 1934, in Mobile, Alabama, one of eight children. Growing up, he liked to hit bottle caps with a broomstick. He helped out his family by earning money by delivering ice in the neighborhood. Aaron believes that lifting the 25-pound blocks of ice helped him develop strong forearms and wrists.

At the age of 16 Aaron began playing ball with the Indianapolis Clowns. The Milwaukee Braves bought Aaron's contract in 1952 and sent him to play in the minor leagues. He hit .336 in his first season and the following season he led his league with a .362 average.

In 1954, when one of the Braves outfielders broke his ankle, Aaron moved up from the minors to take his place. He batted .280 with 13 home runs and 69 RBIs. Then Aaron broke his ankle but came back stronger the next season, hitting .314 with 27 home runs and 106 RBIs. The Braves had found a slugger.

Before hanging up his spikes, Aaron achieved some remarkable feats. He captured the batting crown twice and the slugging crown four times. He led several times each in hits, runs, doubles, and RBIs. He won the Most Valuable Player (MVP) award in 1957 when he hit .322 with 44 home runs and 132 RBIs. In the World Series he hit .393, with three home runs that helped the Braves win the championship in seven games.

THE SLUGGERS

THEY BROKE THEIR RECORDS

Fill in the missing number in this sequence: 762-755-714-____. If you said 138, you're either terrible at math or obscenely good at trivia. In a regressive sequence of home run records, who would ever guess 138 was once a major league record for homers? It's not the numbers that count here – we're looking for names of players who held famous major league records before they were more famously broken.

1. 138. Yes, that was the HR record for twenty-five years, until Babe Ruth shot past the mark midway through a 59-homer season in 1921. The man Ruth surpassed is in the Hall of Fame and hit double-digit dead-ball HRs seven times. He also led the Giants to two championship titles, in 1888 and '89.

2. Angel Francisco Rodriguez saved a record 62 games in 2008. What White Sox closer held the previous single-season record with 57 saves in 1990?

3. In 1961, the MLB career record for games saved was 107, held by former Yankee reliever Johnny Murphy. Fifty years later, another Yankee relief pitcher set a new record with 603 saves. Who is the new record holder, and which fellow 600-save closer saw his record bested a year after his retirement?

4. Pete Rose had a long way to go to top Ty Cobb in hits, but it took Ty nearly two decades to out-hit this NL great. He capped off his twenty-seven-year career in 1897 with 3,435 hits and five pennants won as player-manager for the Chicago White Stockings – yet is known today as the greatest player in Cubs franchise history.

5. In 1925, Tris Speaker broke this man's career record for doubles. Upon his landmark defection from the NL Phillies to the crosstown A's in the new American League, a court injunction forbade the superstar to play anywhere in Philadelphia, so he joined the AL's Cleveland Indians. Thrilled with their new team's acquisition, a newspaper vote by fans chose to rename the team the "Naps."

6. Hack Wilson's 1930 record for RBI in a single season stood for sixty-nine years until a new record was set – by Hack Wilson. Officially upped from 190 to 191, breaking the record of 175 hit by this American League stalwart in 1927. The closest threat to Wilson's mark, 184 ribbies, came the very next season – amassed by very same AL slugger he just surpassed.

7. Candy Cummings. Pud Galvin. Vince DiMaggio. Harmon Killebrew. Bobby Bonds. Adam Dunn. Ryan Howard. Great players courageous enough to reach new depths of human imperfection. Each set new season records for strikeouts, and not the Nolan Ryan kind. Still, none fulfilled the Pre-Columbian prophecy of he who would bring "two centuries of blight" to the record books. But in 2008 a man in Arizona passed a threshold that Howard stopped at with 199 Ks a year prior. But his 204 Ks were not shocking enough – so he smashed his new mark with an unspeakable 223 strikeouts a year later. A 2011 trade to Baltimore allowed him to attain the Junior Circuit record as well.

8. In 1991, Rickey Henderson not only stole his 939th base to break this man's record for career steals, but also literally stole major league property by yanking the base out of its foundation and holding it aloft as a new addition to his personal memorabilia collection.

9. 138 – that number again. Forget homers, it's also the all-time single-season stolen base record in major league history – eight more than Rickey's 130 in 1982. I'll bet you a big nickel you can't name this impish American Association player who nicked this huge total in 1887. Before you give up, remember: correct answer equals huge nickel.

10. 511 wins by Cy Young is, safe to say, unbreakable. But before Denton True could become the greatest hurler in history, he had to make people forget about the future HOFer known as "Gentle Jeems," the first 300-game winner in history. Oh, and we already said he held the record for career strikeouts, not the Nolan Ryan kind.

THEY BROKE THEIR RECORDS (ANSWERS)

1. Roger Connor

2. Bobby Thigpen

3. Mariano Rivera and Trevor Hoffman (#2)

4. Cap Anson

5. Nap Lajoie

6. Lou Gehrig

7. Mark Reynolds

8. Lou Brock

9. Hugh Nicol

10. Pud Galvin

BABE RUTH ★★★ Played 1914–1935

George Herman "Babe" Ruth, also known as "the Bambino" or "the Sultan of Swat," could arguably be the best player ever to play the game. He is first all-time in slugging percentage, eighth all-time in batting average, third in bases on balls, second in runs and RBIs, among the top trio of all-time home run hitters, and incredibly had two 20-win seasons as a pitcher before converting to the outfield. Babe

CAREER STATISTICS	
Batting average	.342
At bats	8,399
Hits	2,873
Doubles	506
Triples	136
Home runs	714
Runs scored	2,174
Runs batted in	2,211
Bases on balls	2,062

was one of the five original inductees into the Baseball Hall of Fame in 1936.

Abandoned by his parents as a youth, Babe Ruth grew to be a much-loved baseball player who changed the face of the game. His feats on the diamond became legendary and he truly fit the mold of an American hero. When Ruth was seven his parents placed him in a school in Baltimore for difficult boys where he trained to be a tailor. To keep the irascible Ruth out of trouble, one of the teachers got him playing baseball. Ruth played all the time, joining several teams, playing every position. Babe's talent earned him a tryout with the Baltimore Orioles. They liked him, signed him, but in 1914 sold him to the Boston Red Sox.

The New York Yankees wanted Babe Ruth, so they bought him for $100,000, a record amount at the time. The Babe went on to create a Yankee dynasty, winning seven pennants and four World Series championships. In 1920, the first year playing for the Yankees, Babe hit 54 home runs; the next year he hit 59 home runs and led the league in nine offensive categories, including an

When he started playing professional baseball, Ruth was a chubby-faced youth. His looks and enthusiasm for the game had his teammates calling him "Baby." Later, it was shortened to "Babe."

eye-popping slugging percentage of .846. Ruth knew how to go out in style too. He blasted his final home runs—numbers 712, 713 and 714—in one game at Forbes Field in Pittsburgh. The last one sailed out of the park, the first time that had ever happened.

THE SLUGGERS

TRIPLE CROWN PITCHERS

These hurlers won the pitching version of the "Triple Crown" by leading their league in wins, strikeouts and earned run average. Name these astounding aces.

1. In 1985, this Met was absolutely surgical on the mound during his sophomore season, winning 24 games, K'ing 268 batters and posting a 1.53 ERA.

2. 1972 saw this lefty win 27 games for a team that won only 59 times. His 1.97 ERA and 310 Ks also topped the NL that year.

3. During his Triple Crown seasons of 1963, '65 and '66, this pitcher averaged 26 wins, 335 Ks and a 1.88 ERA.

4. In 1939, the mound dominance of this Red was enough to win him MVP. In addition to his league-best 27 Ws, 137 Ks and 2.29 ERA, this converted third baseman hit .325 at the plate. These impressive numbers account for the best "Black Ink" stats (Bill James' formula for awarding points to league leaders in various statistical categories) by any pitcher not enshrined in Cooperstown.

5. These two lefties each had two Triple Crown pitching seasons in the American League during the 1930s. One did it as an Athletic in 1930 and '31. The other was a Yankee who dominated the league in 1934 and '37. Name both Hall of Famers.

6. Despite an elderly nickname and pitching for a team of Grays, this twenty-nine-year old was immortal on the mound in 1884. His Providence club played 112 games, 73 of which this HOFer started and finished. He ended with an incredible 59 wins, 441 Ks, 1.38 ERA and a world championship title.

7. In back-to-back seasons, this AL East phenom posted two of the most dominant pitching seasons in history – and he did it during baseball's liveliest hitting era. In 1999, his 23 wins and 313 strikeout totals were league bests, and his 2.07 ERA was more than two full runs lower than the league average.

8. Only Walter Johnson and two others have had three Triple Crown pitching seasons. One we honored above, but this tragic figure dominated the NL in wins, strikeouts and ERA for three seasons between 1915 and 1920, averaging more than 30 wins in his Triple Crown years. Amazingly, that period included two years in Europe fighting in World War I, losing him for most of the 1918 and 1919 seasons. Prior to entering the war, the Cubs picked him up from the Phillies, who had jettisoned the pitcher in fear he would be drafted. He was suffering hearing loss and psychological trauma in France, which fueled his alcoholism. Upon his return to the Cubs in 1920, he posted Triple Crown stats once more before his performance diminished from spectacular to pedestrian for the next decade.

9. A Twin dominated the AL in 2006 to take home his second Cy Young in three years. The Venezuelan lefty topped his league with 19 wins, 245 Ks and a 2.77 ERA that season.

10. 2011 saw perhaps the most dominating pitching season by any pitcher of the twenty-first century. With 24 wins, 250 Ks and a 2.40 ERA – more than a run lower than his career average – he propelled his AL Central team to only their second postseason appearance in twenty-five years.

TRIPLE CROWN PITCHERS (ANSWERS)

1. Dwight Gooden

2. Steve Carlton

3. Sandy Koufax

4. Bucky Walters

5. Lefty Grove and Lefty Gomez

6. Charley "Old Hoss" Radbourn

7. Pedro Martinez

8. Pete Alexander

9. Johan Santana

10. Justin Verlander

WILLIE MAYS ★★★ Played 1951–1973

Willie Howard "Say Hey" Mays hit 660 home runs in his career, hitting over 40 home runs in six seasons and more than 50 in two. He posted a career batting average of .302. He is one of a handful of players to compile 500 home runs and 3,000 hits. Mays was inducted into the Baseball Hall of Fame in 1979.

CAREER STATISTICS

Batting average	.302
At bats	10,881
Hits	3,283
Doubles	523
Triples	140
Home runs	660
Runs scored	2,062
Runs batted in	1,903
Bases on balls	1,463

Willie Mays was born on the edge of Birmingham, Alabama, in the small town of Westfield on May 6, 1931. He was the oldest of 12 children. He came by his athleticism naturally. His mother had been a sprinter and his father played baseball, starring in local league baseball.

Mays played for the Birmingham Barons before signing in 1950 with the New York Giants. In 1951 when he was batting .477 for the Giants' Triple-A team the Giants brought him to the big leagues. Mays had a tough time adjusting to major league pitching, hitting one home run between two hitless streaks of 12 and 13 at bats. Mays

Say Hey Willie earned his nickname because "Say Hey" was his hello to everyone he saw. It covered over Willie's inability to remember people's names.

asked to be sent down but manager Leo Durocher wouldn't hear of it. He loved Willie's spectacular fielding, throwing arm and base running and was certain that his hitting would come around. Durocher's faith in Mays paid off. Despite his difficult start, Mays ended his rookie season with a .274 average and 20 home runs.

In 1954 Mays won the batting crown with a .345 average and the MVP award while slugging 41 home runs. He won the MVP award again in 1965, batting .317 with 52 home runs. Mays was one of the top six vote recipients for the MVP award for 12 years. Mays combined spectacular batting performance and phenomenal fielding with unparalleled showmanship. When he ran the bases his cap flew off and when he caught fly balls he tapped his glove (to signal he had a bead on it) and then made his signature basket catch. And he once caught a 475-foot fly ball to centerfield with his bare hand.

THE SLUGGERS

Managed Two Franchises to World Series

HOF Manager Bill McKechnie won a record three pennants with three separate
franchises – the Pirates, Cardinals and Reds. Similarly, the following skippers also
managed to guide more than one franchise to the World Series. See how many
you can name...

1. He thrice guided Oakland to the Series, but won only once. More recently,
    he managed the Cardinals in three Fall Classics, winning it all in 2006 and
    2011 to become one of two managers to win titles in both leagues.

2. The man known as "Captain Hook" also won World Series in both the NL
    and AL. In the 1970s, he was at the helm for one of history's greatest
    teams, winning Series titles twice. The 1980s brought him a new AL job
    and another title in 1984. His success in each league made him the only
    skipper to have the most managerial wins for two franchises.

3. Like McKechnie, this recent HOF inductee took three franchises to World
    Series, performing near miracles in 1967 and 1984. In between, he
    managed to capture consecutive rings in 1972 and '73.

4. He famously skippered improbable World Series entries with the 1997
    Marlins and 2006 Tigers.

5. This mouthy HOFer dispatched the 1941 Dodgers and two 1950s Giants
    teams from the dugout and into the World Series.

6. He picked up where Miller Huggins left off and won seven more
    championships in the '30s and '40s with the Yankees. Before that, this
    HOFer cut his teeth with the Cubs, leading them to the 1929 pennant.
    Overall, his .615 winning percentage is best all-time amongst managers.

7. This HOFer played nineteen seasons at catcher and, for more than forty
    years, held the record for games caught until being surpassed by Bob
    Boone. As manager, his pennant-winning 1954 Cleveland squad won 111
    regular season games. In 1959, he guided a far less potent White Sox club
    to a surprising pennant victory.

8. This HOF hitter did double duty at age twenty-six as an All-Star shortstop and skipper for the pennant-winning Senators in 1933. He later guided the 1946 Red Sox to 104 regular season wins and an ill-fated World Series appearance against the St. Louis Cardinals.

9. The second man ever to win the Rookie of the Year, "The Swamp Fox" proved a capable manager, leading the 1962 Giants to 103 wins and the pennant at only forty years old. It took him twelve years and three job changes to finally win it all with a ready-made championship outfit in Oakland in 1974.

10. 1926 was an "off year" for this prolific hitter with a .358 career average, but it did not stop him from performing his managerial duties as he led the Cardinals to a World Series victory. Assuming the same player-manager role with the Cubs in 1932, he made up for a career-low .226 average by winning another National League title.

MANAGED TWO FRANCHISES TO WORLD SERIES (ANSWERS)

1. Tony La Russa

2. Sparky Anderson

3. Dick Williams

4. Jim Leyland

5. Leo Durocher

6. Joe McCarthy

7. Al Lopez

8. Joe Cronin

9. Alvin Dark

10. Rogers Hornsby

FOUR OR FEWER LETTERS, 40 HR

When Adam Dunn started dumping more than 40 home runs into stands five straight years starting in 2004, he ruined a good trivia question. It used to be there were only ten men in history to hit at least 40 homers in at least one season and have four or fewer letters in their last name. Let's step back into the twentieth century and find out who they were...

1. "The Big Cat" went for 40 or more three times with the Cardinals and Giants in his Hall of Fame career.
2. He yanked 40 an amazing eleven times.
3. This bestial Athletic and Red Sox slammed 40 or more five times.
4. In the big AL home run year of 1961, this Tiger deposited 41 home runs into the stands. His total ranked only sixth in the league – but enough to include him in this trivial trust.
5. Name the recent Hall of Fame inductee who totaled an amazing 406 bases in 1978, 184 of which came via monstrous home runs (do the math). It was the only 40-plus home run season of his career – though he hit exactly 39 three other times.
6. The smallest member of the 500 HR club, this "Giant" lefty found a technique of wrapping taters around the short right field pole at his home Polo Grounds. Appropriately, his last name is also the shortest in this category.
7. He ordered up a league MVP award by smacking 47 homers as a Blue Jay in 1987.
8. This HOFer was very familiar with outfield dimensions, winning twelve straight Gold Gloves in center. He also sent out at least 40 round-trippers five times.
9. 1955 was an anomaly for this Red when he knocked exactly 40 HRs over walls and had 109 RBI with a .309 batting average, all career highs. Somewhere in this question are clues to his name, the most obscure of the category's answers.
10. This Cub is one of only eight sluggers to have hit 600 home runs. He hit more than 40 in a season seven times, and topped 60 thrice.

FOUR OR FEWER LETTERS, 40 HR (ANSWERS)

1. Johnny Mize

2. Babe Ruth

3. Jimmie Foxx

4. Norm Cash

5. Jim Rice

6. Mel Ott

7. George Bell

8. Willie Mays

9. Wally Post

10. Sammy Sosa

HALL OF FAMER HOME STATES (1ST INNING)

Each group of Hall of Famers below has something in common: they were all born in the same state. Name that state.

1. Ty Cobb, Josh Gibson, Jackie Robinson

2. Joe DiMaggio, Ted Williams, Tony Gwynn

3. Lou Gehrig, Frankie Frisch, Sandy Koufax

4. Kirby Puckett, Bill Veeck, Charlie Comiskey

5. Ernie Banks, Rogers Hornsby, Tris Speaker

6. Bill Dickey, Ted Lyons, Mel Ott

7. Nap Lajoie, Gabby Hartnett, Hugh Duffy

8. Hank Aaron, Willie Mays, Billy Williams, Ozzie Smith, Satchel Paige

9. Cap Anson, Bob Feller, Dazzy Vance

10. Cy Young, Branch Rickey, Mike Schmidt, Kenesaw Mountain Landis

HALL OF FAMER HOME STATES (1ST INNING ANSWERS)

1. Georgia

2. California

3. New York

4. Illinois

5. Texas

6. Louisiana

7. Rhode Island

8. Alabama

9. Iowa

10. Ohio

STADIUMS OF YESTERYEAR

Very simply, name the franchises that played at these old homes. Note: 10 is still in use, though under a different name.

1. Ebbets Field

2. Polo Grounds (3 teams)

3. Navin Field

4. Crosley Field

5. Forbes Field

6. Jarry Park

7. Sicks Stadium

8. Shibe Park (2 teams)

9. The Kingdome

10. Weeghman Park

STADIUMS OF YESTERYEAR (ANSWERS)

1. Brooklyn Dodgers

2. Giants, Yankees, Mets

3. Detroit Tigers

4. Cincinnati Reds

5. Pittsburgh Pirates

6. Montreal Expos

7. Seattle Pilots

8. Philadelphia A's and Phillies

9. Seattle Mariners

10. Chicago Cubs – Originally built for the Chicago Whales of the
    –ill-fated Federal League, Weeghman was renovated in the
    1920s and properly renamed for team owner Wrigley for the
    1927 season, during which the Cubs became the first-ever
    Senior Circuit franchise to draw one million fans (Babe Ruth
    brought more than one million to the Polo Grounds in his first
    year with the Yankees).

FAMOUS TRADES (1ST INNING)

Name the notable but unnamed players traded on the following dates.

1. November 2, 1974: Home run great is traded by the Atlanta Braves to the Milwaukee Brewers for a player to be named and Dave May.

2. May 25, 1984: Future HOF reliever is traded by the Boston Red Sox with Mike Brumley to the Chicago Cubs for Bill Buckner.

3. December 10, 1935: All-time great is traded by the Philadelphia Athletics with Johnny Marcum to the Boston Red Sox for Gordon Rhodes, George Savino and $150,000.

4. March 30, 1992: Fateful Windy City deal goes down when Cubs trade George Bell to the Chicago White Sox for Ken Patterson and this weak-hitting outfielder with a .376 slugging average.

5. January 23, 1981: Red Sox send this All-Star OF with Steve Renko to the California Angels for Frank Tanana, Jim Dorsey and Joe Rudi.

6. November 3, 1992: New York Yankees acquire right field fixture for future title teams from Cincinnati Reds for Roberto Kelly.

7. July 31, 1997: He's sent by Oakland Athletics to St. Louis Cardinals for Eric Ludwick, T.J. Mathews and Blake Stein.

8. October 25, 1973: Slugger is swapped by the San Francisco Giants with Bernard Williams to the San Diego Padres for Mike Caldwell.

9. December 5, 1990: The Toronto Blue Jays trade this slugger with Tony Fernandez to the San Diego Padres for Joe Carter and this future HOF second baseman.

10. November 13, 1996: He's traded by the San Francisco Giants to Cleveland for Jeff Kent, Julian Tavarez and Jose Vizcaino.

Famous Trades (1st Inning answers)

1. Hank Aaron

2. Dennis Eckersley

3. Jimmie Foxx

4. Sammy Sosa

5. Fred Lynn

6. Paul O'Neill

7. Mark McGwire

8. Willie McCovey

9. Fred McGriff and Roberto Alomar

10. Matt Williams

500TH HOME RUNS

Name these members of the 500 HR club. You're given years and the name of the pitcher who served up the pitch to make these special moments possible.

1. June 20, 2004: Meteoric early career in which this moment was predicted much earlier finally happens with HR off Matt Morris.
2. Bud Black blanked the Angels over eight innings on September 17, 1984, giving up only three hits. But one of those hits was this man's 500th career home run.
3. On September 24, 1940, he hit his 500th against George Caster from the A's, the team he starred with for a decade before joining the Red Sox.
4. April 18, 1987: No window dressing here. Top of the ninth, 2 outs, Pirates 6, Phillies 5. This man hit No. 500 off Don Robinson, a three-run job that won the game.
5. Addled by injury in the twilight of his career, a Yankees legend connects for his 500th off Oriole Stu Miller on May 14, 1967.
6. Two months later, July 14, 1967: Juan Marichal gives up a home run to this man, who, after a great career with the Braves, was in an Astros uniform when he hit his milestone bomb.
7. Exactly one year later, the former teammate of the last man hit his 500th HR off another Giant, Mike McCormick. But No. 500 was a mere pit stop during this prodigious slugger's career.
8. September 13, 1971: This Oriole hit No. 499 in the first game of a doubleheader, then hit No. 500 in the second game off Fred Scherman.
9. Still skilled at age forty-one, this man sent his historic shot off Cleveland pitcher Wynn Hawkins on June 17, 1960, to become the oldest player ever to hit a 500th HR.
10. Amongst this select club, it took this man the most at-bats (11,095) to reach 500. But steady slugging over twenty-one years made No. 500 possible off Felipe Lira in 1996.

500TH HOME RUNS (ANSWERS)

1. Ken Griffey Jr.

2. Reggie Jackson

3. Jimmie Foxx

4. Mike Schmidt

5. Mickey Mantle

6. Eddie Matthews

7. Hank Aaron

8. Frank Robinson

9. Ted Williams

10. Eddie Murray

THREE-OUTFIELDER MONTE

Keep your eye on the question mark. Which outfielder is missing from these notable teams? Year, team, most frequent outfield mates.

1. 2008 Philadelphia Phillies – LF?, CF Shane Victorino, RF Jayson Werth

2. 2004 Boston Red Sox – LF Manny Ramirez, CF?, RF Gabe Kapler

3. 1996 New York Yankees – LF Gerald Williams, CF Bernie Williams, RF?

4. 1989 Oakland A's – LF?, CF Dave Henderson, RF Stan Javier

5. 1987 Toronto Blue Jays – LF George Bell, CF Lloyd Moseby, RF?

6. 2005 Chicago White Sox – LF Scott Podsednik, CF Aaron Rowand, RF?

7. 1969 New York Mets – LF Cleon Jones, CF?, RF Ron Swoboda

8. 1987 Minnesota Twins – LF Dan Gladden, CF Kirby Puckett, RF?

9. 1984 Chicago Cubs – LF Gary Matthews, CF?, RF Keith Moreland

10. 1975 Cincinnati Reds – LF George Foster, CF Cesar Geronimo, RF?

11. 1986 Houston Astros – LF Jose Cruz, CF Billy Hatcher, RF?

12. 1927 New York Yankees – LF?, CF Earle Combs, RF Babe Ruth

THREE-OUTFIELDER MONTE (ANSWERS)

1. LF Pat Burrell

2. CF Johnny Damon

3. RF Paul O'Neill

4. LF Rickey Henderson

5. RF Jesse Barfield

6. RF Jermaine Dye

7. CF Tommie Agee

8. RF Tom Brunansky

9. CF Bob Dernier

10. RF Ken Griffey

11. RF Kevin Bass

12. LF Bob Meusel

TY COBB ★★★ Played 1905–1928

Ty Cobb may be the greatest hitter to play the game. He holds the all-time record for batting average, with .367, is second in runs, second in hits and triples and fourth in doubles and fifth in RBIs. For all but one of the 13 years between 1907 and 1919, he captured the batting title. He was the top vote recipient on the first Baseball Hall of Fame ballot, beating out Babe Ruth and Honus Wagner.

CAREER STATISTICS

Batting average	.367
At bats	11,429
Hits	4,191
Doubles	724
Triples	297
Home runs	118
Runs scored	2,245
Runs batted in	1,961
Bases on balls	1,249

Ty Cobb was the best offensive player of the Dead Ball era. In the early years of the 20th century home runs were scarce. Batters relied on careful hit placement, bunts, steals, and hit-and-run plays to move around the bases and score runs. Ty Cobb was a master of these tactics. Cobb's batting prowess and lifetime batting average of .367 is likely to stand forever. Players today rarely average in a season what Cobb averaged in a lifetime.

Cobb compiled nine 200-hit seasons. For three seasons, he batted over .400. Starting in his second year, and for 22 years after that, Cobb batted over .300. He even managed to take the Triple Crown in 1909, with a .377 average, nine home runs, and 107 RBIs. Cobb was an extraordinary base-stealer, often stealing second,

Despite his achievements, Cobb's Detroit Tigers went in 1909 to its only World Series, which they lost. It is Cobb's biggest regret that he wasn't on a World Championship team.

third and home. When asked what he did when he saw Cobb stealing second, one catcher replied, "I throw to third."

Cobb disliked the way Babe Ruth had changed the game with his prodigious slugging of home runs. Cobb believed it took more batting skill—and that the game was more interesting—if players hit line drives into the outfield gaps. In 1925 Cobb announced he would be a power hitter for two games to prove how easy it was to hit home runs. In the first game, he hit three home runs. In the second game he hit two. Satisfied that he had proved his point, he went back to slapping singles and rifling doubles between the outfielders.

THE HITTERS

TWENTY-GAME LOSERS

Winning 20 games is a mark of distinction in baseball, as is the even rarer feat of losing 20 games. But where "distinction" connotes merit in the former case, the latter carries a more regrettable implication. Even so, the 20-loss seasons posted by the following pitchers are especially remarkable. Name these dubious moundsmen.

1. 1974 saw five 20-game losers – the most in baseball since 1920. Interestingly, four of these pitchers were All-Stars at one point in their careers, and three of them won 20 games, another 19. You only need to name the one of this bunch who won more than 200 games and a World Series MVP Award for being the last man to pitch three complete game wins in the Fall Classic.

2. This HOF pitcher both won and lost 20 games for Atlanta in 1979.

3. In 1973, this knuckle-balling White Sox lefty had 18 wins at the All-Star Break, but didn't make the All-Star team – perhaps because he had 14 losses as well. He finished the season 24-20.

4. A former ROY with the New York Mets performed the rare 20-wins-one-year, 20-losses-the-next in 1976-77, this feat from a man who years earlier was on the mound to retire the last batter in Game 5 of the Miracle Mets' 1969 World Series Championship.

5. After factoring in nearly half of his team's wins in 1972 en route to a Cy Young Award for a last-place team, this ascetic ace went 13-20 the following year.

6. This man went an abysmal 3-21 for the 1954 Orioles. Two years later, with the Yankees, he pitched a fairly memorable World Series win.

7. No stranger to 20 losses in a career that spanned four decades, this colorful pitcher is one of only two men to win 200-plus games and lose more games (222) than he won (211). Many of those losses came with the Senators, a team he played for in five separate stints, prompting his quip about serving more terms in Washington than President Franklin Roosevelt.

8. On his way to becoming the second-winningest pitcher of all time, this hurler was still perfecting his craft at age twenty-one when he went 13-25 in 1909.

9. For more than two decades, this man proudly wore the crown as MLB's last 20-game loser, a feat he achieved with the Oakland A's in 1980. That one year featured the bulk of decisions in his five-season span where his winning percentage was .338 (23 wins, 45 losses).

10. On a team that lost 119 games in 2003, this young Tiger absorbed 21 of those defeats, much to the chagrin of the man in the previous question.

TWENTY-GAME LOSERS (ANSWERS)

1.   Mickey Lolich

2.   Phil Niekro

3.   Wilbur Wood

4.   Jerry Koosman

5.   Steve Carlton

6.   Don Larsen

7.   Bobo Newsom

8.   Walter Johnson

9.   Brian Kingman

10.   Mike Maroth

TED WILLIAMS ★★★ Played 1939–1960

Theodore Samuel "the Splendid Splinter" Williams was the last man ever to exceed the .400 batting average mark. Only once in his 19-year career did he hit under .300, and he won six batting titles and two Triple Crowns. He also led the league four times each in home runs and RBIs. He retired with a .344 batting average, putting him fifth on the all-time list. He was inducted into the Baseball Hall of Fame in 1966.

CAREER STATISTICS

Batting average	.344
At bats	7,706
Hits	2,654
Doubles	525
Triples	71
Home runs	521
Runs scored	1,798
Runs batted in	1,839
Bases on balls	2,019

Born on August 30, 1918, in San Diego, California, Ted Williams had a difficult childhood. His mother was a devoted Salvation Army follower, regularly leaving her children home alone and often enlisting Ted to march in the band with her, much to the young boy's embarrassment. His father abandoned the family. Fortunately, Ted had an outlet. It was baseball. Day after day in sunny California he could be found on the sandlots of San Diego, honing the sweetest swing that baseball ever saw.

Eddie Collins, a former great hitter and then the general manager of the Boston Red Sox, discovered Ted's talents. Collins was in San Diego scouting Bobby Doerr when he saw a hitter taking batting practice with the most perfect swing he'd ever seen. It was Ted Williams. Collins signed him immediately.

In 1939, William's rookie season with the Red Sox, the cocksure Teddy Ballgame (a name he called himself) hit .327, clouted 31 home runs and compiled 145 RBIs, tops in the league. The next year Williams batted .344 and in 1941 he hit .406, the last time anyone has batted over .400 in the major leagues. In 18 of his 19 years in the big leagues, Williams batted over .300. His final season, in 1960, he batted .316 and slugged 29 home runs in a mere 113 games. At age 42, the legendary Teddy Ballgame, a.k.a. The Kid and The Thumper, not only hit safely three out of ten times but also slammed a home run three times among his every ten base hits. Amazing!

THE HITTERS

RIBBIE RECORDS

This category seeks to acknowledge players who've led their league in RBI multiple times. No small feat, leading the league in RBI often signals clutch hitting, robust power or MVP performance. Name these players.

1. Fire-hydrant-ish Cub is famous for his record 191 RBI season in 1930, which was a follow up to his league-leading 159 RBI season in '29. What's his name?

2. Another Cubs slugger deserves mention for leading the NL in home runs and majors in RBI during the two war seasons of 1943 and '44. "Swish" was a five-time All-Star who never batted in more than 100 runs other than those two seasons.

3. While the last man was leading the depleted NL in RBI in 1943, this man was knocking in a league-leading 109 ribbies for the Browns in the AL. Proving that year was no fluke, he again topped the AL in 1949 and '50 with 159 and 144 RBI, respectively, as a slugging shortstop with the Red Sox. Can you name this should-be Hall of Famer?

4. Along with leading the NL in homers five times during the dead-ball 1910s, this early Phillies star led his league in RBI in 1913 and the franchise's first pennant year of 1915. Can you name this oddly-dubbed outfielder with three "V"s in his name?

5. While the last man wasn't leading the NL in RBI, this teammate often was. Four times in twelve years he topped the NL – but never consecutively. A glass of sweet wine should help you relax and elicit an answer to this one.

6. Having Ty Cobb, Sam Crawford and Harry Heilmann on base all the time gave this cleanup hitter plenty of RBI opportunities. Three times he led the AL in RBI, including a league-low record 78 RBI. AYU will vouch for your trivia supremacy if you can get this one...

7. Speaking of 78, 1978 was the last of three consecutive years this Red led his league in RBI. You may remember him as the only man to hit 50 homers in that decade...

8. He was an All-American halfback at California before leading the American League in RBI three times in the 1950s. Famous for his fear of flying, it didn't keep him from winning the 1958 MVP with the Red Sox. Name this alliterative athlete.

9. After honing his skills in Japan, "Big Daddy" came back to terrorize AL pitchers and lead the league in RBI every year from 1990 to 1992. Name this tubby Tiger.

10. Fans will remember this catching great for lubricating the flow of his team's run production. Every other year from 1970 to 1975, he led the NL in RBI. Close out the category by batting in a correct answer.

RIBBIE RECORDS (ANSWERS)

1. Hack Wilson

2. Bill Nicholson

3. Vern Stephens

4. Gavvy Cravath

5. Sherry Magee

6. Bobby Veach

7. George Foster

8. Jackie Jensen

9. Cecil Fielder

10. Johnny Bench

BASEBALL LINEAGES: DODGERS CATCHERS

Perhaps no other position on the field is more valuable to maintaining team continuity than a franchise catcher. History shows that behind every great dynasty is a great catcher. The Dodgers franchise has a lineage of exceptional catchers throughout their history. We've created a timeline of primary catchers over the past half century, and ask you to name some of the more prominent ones. Put the pudges in their proper place to complete the pedigree puzzle.

BROOKLYN/L.A. DODGERS CATCHERS			
YEARS	CATCHER	YEARS	CATCHER
1948-57	1.?	1981-92	4.?
		1993-97	5.?
1958-67	2.?	1998	C. Johnson
		1999-00	Todd Hundley
		2001-04	6.?
		2005	J. Phillips
1968-70	Tom Haller	2006-10	7.?
1971-73	3 Catchers	2011	Rod Barajas
1974-80	3.?		

BASEBALL LINEAGES: DODGERS CATCHERS (ANSWERS)

1. Roy Campanella

2. John Roseboro

3. Steve Yeager

4. Mike Scioscia

5. Mike Piazza

6. Paul Lo Duca

7. Russell Martin

BOXSCORE ABBREVIATIONS

Brush up on your boxscore-keeping skills by identifying what these official scoring abbreviations represent.

1. A

2. HBP

3. GIDP

4. SF

5. CS

6. K

7. Reversed K

8. BK

9. TP

10. FC

11. I2

12. What defensive number is the catcher assigned for purposes of official scoring?

BOXSCORE ABBREVIATIONS (ANSWERS)

1. Assist

2. Hit by pitch

3. Grounded into double play

4. Sacrifice fly

5. Caught stealing

6. Strikeout

7. Called third strike (caught "looking" without swinging)

8. Balk

9. Triple play

10. Fielder's choice

11. Catcher's interference

12. 2

BASEBALL BEFORE AND AFTER

This category asks you to name two baseball figures who share a common name. The answer to the first part of the clue will have a last name that overlaps with the first name of the second half of the clue. For example:

> Q: K-King meets Phillies 2006 MVP slugger
> A: Nolan Ryan Howard

Get it? Great, now get to it while the getting's good.

1. Space man meets 478 career saves

2. Pitcher's eponymous surgery meets Little Napoleon with NL managerial wins record

3. Bespectacled integration GM meets steals king

4. Pine tar meltdown meets coffee-crazed Punch and Judy hitter who frankly doesn't give a damn

5. Hammerin' Hank meets he who won 2003 ALCS for Yankees with eleventh-inning HR

6. Split-finger maestro who won 1986 Cy Young and NLCS MVP (despite losing) meets '98 World Series MVP at 3B

7. Cheeseburger was left on third base for this portly ump from Philly meets former first-round pick (no. 20 overall) who began his fourteen-year career with Mets in 1987 and was known for increasing his bat speed by swinging underwater.

8. 1964 AL MVP with most Gold Gloves by non-pitcher meets Yanks' Silver Slugging All-Star incumbent at second

9. "Lefty"-philic fans filled Vet for this Phobic Phillie ace meets Fall Classic's fair ball-willing backstop

10. Gold Glove left fielder on A's title teams of 1970s meets Tigers' perennial 1940s All-Star at 1B who forced Greenberg to outfield

BASEBALL BEFORE AND AFTER (ANSWERS)

1. Bill **Lee** Smith

2. Tommy **John** McGraw

3. Branch **Rickey** Henderson

4. George **Brett** Butler

5. Hank **Aaron** Boone

6. Mike **Scott** Brosius

7. Eric **Gregg** Jefferies

8. Brooks **Robinson** Cano

9. Steve **Carlton** Fisk

10. Joe **Rudi** York

BACK-TO-BACK BATTING TITLES

The home run ball had an ugly adolescence before becoming a statistical celebrity in the 1920s. Home runs were less a measure of Herculean strength than cheap consequence of indiscriminate field dimensions or simply a "ground-rule double" that then counted as four bases. The greatest players of the early twentieth century were known for their batting average. Nap Lajoie, Honus Wagner, Ty Cobb and Rogers Hornsby each won a slew of batting titles, and did so consecutively for several years. In the decades since Hornsby set a record for six straight seasons leading the NL in batting, only a handful of hitters have won batting titles in consecutive seasons. See how many of back-to-back batting champs you can name using their team, position and title years. Note: In some cases, such as Question 12, the player won the batting title in additional years.

1. New York Giants (1B) – 1930, 1931

2. Philadelphia A's (OF) – 1930, 1931

3. St. Louis Cardinals (OF/1B) – 1950, 1951, 1952

4. Philadelphia A's (1B) – 1951, 1952

5. Los Angeles Dodgers (OF) – 1962, 1963

6. Pittsburgh Pirates (RF) –1964, 1965

7. Minnesota Twins (RF) – 1964, 1965

8. Minnesota Twins (2B/1B) – 1972, '73, '74, '75 and 1977, '78

9. Chicago Cubs (3B) – 1975, 1976

10. Pittsburgh Pirates (RF) – 1977, 1978

11. Boston Red Sox (3B) – 1985, '86, '87, '88

12. San Diego Padres (RF) – 1987, '88, '89 and 1994, '95, '96, '97

13. Colorado Rockies (RF) – 1998, 1999

14. Boston Red Sox (SS) – 1999, 2000

15. Minnesota Twins (C) – 2008, 2009

BACK-TO-BACK BATTING TITLES (ANSWERS)

1. Bill Terry (tied at .349 with Cardinal Chick Hafey in 1931)

2. Al Simmons

3. Stan Musial

4. Ferris Fain

5. Tommy Davis

6. Roberto Clemente

7. Tony Oliva

8. Rod Carew

9. Bill Madlock

10. Dave Parker

11. Wade Boggs

12. Tony Gwynn

13. Larry Walker

14. Nomar Garciaparra

15. Joe Mauer

STAN MUSIAL ★★★ Played 1941–1963

Stanley Frank "Stan the Man" Musial is one of the top hitters the game of baseball has ever seen. He is fourth on the all-time total-hits list, third on the doubles list, eighth on the runs scored list, and sixth on the RBI list. He had 18 seasons batting over .300, and he retired with a career batting average of .331. Musial was inducted into the Baseball Hall of Fame in 1969.

CAREER STATISTICS

Batting average	.331
At bats	10,972
Hits	3,630
Doubles	725
Triples	177
Home runs	475
Runs scored	1,949
Runs batted in	1,951
Bases on balls	1,599

"Stan the Man" Musial began his baseball career in 1940 as a pitcher in the St. Louis Cardinal minor leagues. He was pitching and batting well. On one of his off days, he was playing outfield and dove to make a catch, injuring his pitching arm. That marked the end of his pitching career and the beginning of a legendary career as regular position player and extraordinary batter.

The Cardinals put Musial in the outfield and for the first 17 years of his play in the major leagues he hit over .300 (his first season he batted .426, but he only played in 12 games). At the end of 22 years Musial was still a Cardinal, and he had notched 3,630 hits, hit 475 home runs, won seven batting titles, and had six 200-hit seasons.

Musial lost one playing year to World War II, serving in 1945 with the navy. He came back in 1946, won the batting title with a .365 average and also led the league in hits, on-base average, doubles, triples and runs. In 1948 Musial missed the Triple Crown by one home run. He officially

Musial ended his career with his 3,630 hits divided equally between his home and away games. For each he had 1,815 hits.

had 39 that year, but he actually had hit the one more the needed in a game that got rained out. It was also the year that he went 5-for-5 against the Dodgers in one game, and 11-or-15 in that entire series. Of those 11, four were doubles, one was a triple and one was a home run. In 1954, in a doubleheader against the Giants at the Polo Grounds Musial hit five home runs.

THE HITTERS

BASEBALL LINEAGES: GIANTS FIRST BASEMEN

From their start in 1883, the Giants franchise has fielded a litany of Hall of Famers, All-Stars, Silver Sluggers and Gold Glovers at the first base position. Guess the names of the Giant greats gone from this gilded genealogy...

NEW YORK/SAN FRANCISCO GIANTS FIRST BASEMEN			
YEARS	FIRST BASEMAN	YEARS	FIRST BASEMAN
1883-89	1.?	1910-16	2.?
		1917-18	Walter Holke
1890	Dude Esterbrook	1919	Hal Chase
1891			
1892	Buck Ewing		
1893			
1894-95	Dirty Jack Doyle	1920-26	3.?
1896-87	Willie Clark		
1898-1900	Dirty Jack Doyle		
1901	John Ganzel		
1902-07	Dan McGann	1927-36	4.?
1908-09	Fred Tenney	1937-41	3 players

NEW YORK/SAN FRANCISCO GIANTS FIRST BASEMEN			
YEARS	**FIRST BASEMAN**	**YEARS**	**FIRST BASEMAN**
1942			
1943-45	2 players	1981-85	5 players
1946-49	**5.?**		
1950	Tookie Gilbert	1986-93	**9.?**
1951-57	**6.?**		
		1994	Todd Benzinger
		1995-96	Mark Carreon
1958-64	**7.?**	1997-2005	**10.?**
1965-73	**8.?**		
		2006-09	4 players
1974-76	3 players	2010-11	**11.?**
1977-80			

BASEBALL LINEAGES: GIANTS FIRST BASEMEN (ANSWERS)

1. Roger Connor

2. Fred Merkle

3. High Pockets Kelly

4. Bill Terry

5. Johnny Mize

6. Whitey Lockman

7. Orlando Cepeda

8. Willie McCovey

9. Will Clark

10. J.T. Snow

11. Aubrey Huff

MVP FIRSTS

Previous incarnations of the Most Valuable Player Award included the "Chalmers Award" from 1911 to 1914, where MVPs were chosen in both leagues and bestowed a "30 Roadster" – a car 1911 AL winner Ty Cobb already owned – from Chalmers Automotive in Detroit. The stipulation that a player couldn't win more than one Chalmers Award contributed to it falling out of favor. The MVP concept was resurrected under less certified standards in the 1920s, but not until the Baseball Writers' Association of America established set guidelines for MVP voting in 1931 did the idea take hold. These questions relate to seminal moments in MVP voting since 1931.

1. The first AL winner was this Philadelphia Athletics pitcher who led his team to a pennant with a stellar 31-4, 2.06 ERA season in 1931.

2. For trivia's sake, you must know the first NL winner, a Bronx-born Fordham product who bested his AL counterpart in the postseason as the Cardinals defeated Philadelphia in the 1931 World Series.

3. Prior to expansion, the eight teams in each league were sorted into "first" and "second" divisions according to their record – 1 through 4 finishers in the former, 5-8 in the latter. Name the Cub OF who, in 1952, became the first player from a second-division team to win the MVP with 37 HRs and 121 RBI.

4. In 1934, this Tiger HOFer became the first catcher to win the award.

5. This A's slugger was the first two-time MVP winner, the first three-time MVP winner and the first MVP in consecutive years (1932-33).

6. Can you name the Dodgers pitcher who, in 1956, became the first man to win the MVP and the Cy Young in the same year?

7. Who's the only player to win the MVP in both leagues? What teams did he play for when he won them?

8. Ichiro Suzuki won MVP as a "rookie" in 2001. This was the second time a first-year player was awarded the honor. Who was the first?

9. In 1971, this A's pitcher became the youngest-ever recipient of the MVP Award. Name the ace.

10. It's rare for a hurler to win the award, never mind a pitcher coming out of the bullpen. Phillie Jim Konstanty was the first reliever to win it in 1950. Who was the first American League relief pitcher to win MVP? (Hint: It happened in the strike-shortened season of 1981.)

MVP FIRSTS (ANSWERS)

1. Lefty Grove

2. Frankie Frisch

3. Hank Sauer

4. Mickey Cochrane

5. Jimmie Foxx

6. Don Newcombe

7. Frank Robinson (Reds in 1961, Orioles in 1966)

8. Fred Lynn (1975)

9. Vida Blue

10. Rollie Fingers

GREAT LEFTY/RIGHTY COMBOS

The 2001 World Champion Diamondbacks rocketed to a title with a killer lefty/righty duo of Randy Johnson and Curt Schilling. The two shared Series MVP honors for their combined efforts in mowing down Yankee batters. But their time together was fleeting compared to some of the following LH/RH pitching partners who combined for at least 250 wins while on the same roster (Johnson/Schilling had only 145). For each pair of aces, we list their teams and individual win totals. Name these one-two punches throwing from opposite stances on the rubber.

1. Brooklyn/Los Angeles Dodgers, 1956-66, LH 163/RH 177

2. Atlanta Braves, 1988-2008, LH 242/RH 210 (their 452 combined wins is a record for L/R duos)

3. Boston Braves (NL)/Milwaukee Braves, 1951-1963, LH 264/RH 179

4. New York Giants, 1904-1914, LH 138/RH 297

5. New York Yankees, 1930-1942, LH 189/RH 219

6. Detroit Tigers, 1939-1952, LH 200/RH 161

7. Philadelphia Phillies, 1948-1960, LH 114/RH 233

8. New York Mets, 1967-1977, LH 137/RH 189

9. Baltimore Orioles, 1975-1985, LH 129, RH 139

10. Kansas City Royals, 1974-1983, LH 125/RH 136

GREAT LEFTY/RIGHTY COMBOS (ANSWERS)

1. Sandy Koufax and Don Drysdale

2. Tom Glavine and John Smoltz (yes, more than Glavine/Greg Maddux)

3. Warren Spahn and Lew Burdette

4. Hooks Wiltse and Christy Mathewson

5. Lefty Gomez and Red Ruffing

6. Hal Newhouser and Dizzy Trout

7. Curt Simmons and Robin Roberts

8. Jerry Koosman and Tom Seaver

9. Mike Flanagan and Jim Palmer

10. Paul Splittorff and Dennis Leonard

TEAMS THEY PITCHED FOR (1ST INNING)

The following distinguished pitchers were much traveled, playing for different teams with various degrees of success. Each had remarkable stints with at least three squads. Your job: name at least three of those teams for which they pitched. An extra point for each team you can name past three.

1. Nolan Ryan

2. Gaylord Perry

3. Dennis Eckersley

4. Ferguson Jenkins

5. Lee Smith

6. Steve Carlton

7. Pedro Martinez

8. Jerry Reuss

9. Fernando Valenzuela

10. Pete Alexander

TEAMS THEY PITCHED FOR (1ST INNING ANSWERS)

1. Mets, Angels, Astros, Rangers

2. Giants, Indians, Rangers, Padres, Yankees, Braves, Mariners, Royals

3. Indians, Red Sox, Cubs, A's, Cardinals

4. Phillies, Cubs, Rangers, Red Sox

5. Cubs, Red Sox, Cardinals, Yankees, Orioles, Angels, Expos, Reds

6. Cardinals, Phillies, Giants, White Sox, Indians, Twins

7. Dodgers, Expos, Red Sox, Mets, Phillies

8. Dodgers, Pirates, Cardinals, Astros, White Sox, Angels, Reds, Brewers

9. Dodgers, Angels, Orioles, Phillies, Padres, Cardinals

10. Phillies, Cubs, Cardinals

MVP / CY YOUNG TEAMMATES

	Year	Team	MVP (Avg./HRs/RBI)	Cy Young
1.	2006	Twins	.321/34/130	19-6, 2.77, 245 K
2.	2002	Athletics	.308/34/131	23-5, 2.75, 182 K
3.	1991	Braves	.319/22/86	20-11, 2.55, 192 K
4.	1990	Athletics	.325/28/61	27-6, 2.95, 127 K
5.	1990	Pirates	.301/33/114	22-6, 2.76, 131 K
6.	1988	Dodgers	.290/25/76	23-8, 2.26, 178 K
7.	1984	Cubs	.314/19/84	16-1, 2.69, 155 K
8.	1982	Brewers	.331/29/114	18-6, 3.34, 105 K
9.	1980	Phillies	.286/48/121	24-9, 2.34, 286 K
10.	1967	Red Sox	.326/44/121	22-9, 3.16, 246 K
11.	1960	Pirates	.325/2/50	20-9, 3.08, 120 K
12.	1957	Mil. Braves	.322/44/132	21-11, 2.69, 111 K

MVP/Cy Young Teammates (answers)

	MVP	Cy Young
1.	Justin Morneau	Johan Santana
2.	Miguel Tejada	Barry Zito
3.	Terry Pendleton	Tom Glavine
4.	Rickey Henderson	Bob Welch
5.	Barry Bonds	Doug Drabek
6.	Kirk Gibson	Orel Hershiser
7.	Ryne Sandberg	Rick Sutcliffe
8.	Robin Yount	Pete Vuckovich
9.	Mike Schmidt	Steve Carlton
10.	Carl Yastrzemski	Jim Lonborg
11.	Dick Groat	Vern Law
12.	Hank Aaron	Warren Spahn

FRANK ROBINSON ★★★ Played 1956–1976

CAREER STATISTICS

Frank Robinson is ninth on the all-time home-run list, with 586. In 17 of his 21 seasons, he hit more than 20 home runs. He led the American League as a Baltimore Oriole in 1966 with 49. That year he won the Triple Crown and the MVP award, the first player to win an MVP award in each league. He was inducted into the Baseball Hall of Fame in 1982.

Batting average	.294
At bats	10,006
Hits	2,943
Doubles	528
Home runs	586
Runs scored	1,829
Runs batted in	1,812
Bases on balls	1,420

Frank Robinson began his major league career with the Cincinnati Reds in 1956. It was a good start. He led the league with 122 runs, and slugged 38 home runs while batting .290, a performance that earned him the Rookie of the Year award. He consistently hit for power, belting over 30 home runs for ten of his seasons. And he averaged more than .300 nine times.

In 1961 Robinson and the Reds won the pennant. That year Frank led the league in slugging average, and hit .323, with 37 home runs and 124 RBI. He won his first MVP award. Except for a dip in his numbers in 1963, Robinson continued to put in an all-star performance. However, in 1966 the Reds general manager traded Robinson to the Baltimore Orioles where he promptly won another MVP award. He led the Orioles to the American League pennant and World Series, hitting two home runs in the Series as they defeated the Los Angeles Dodgers in four games.

In 1975, Robinson began his managerial career with the Cleveland Indians, becoming baseball's first black manager, 28 years after Jackie Robinson (no relation) broke baseball's color barrier. Robinson was one of the last few player/managers. In his first game as a player/manager Robinson smacked a home run. In 1976, just 57 short of 3,000 hits, he took himself out of the everyday lineup.

In his rookie year, Frank Robinson, who took a batting stance very close to the plate, had the distinction of being the player who was hit by the most pitches (20). In his career, he was struck 198 times.

THE SLUGGERS

BLACK PIONEERS

The following questions test your knowledge on the career of Jackie Robinson and other African-American ballplayers, including several Negro League superstars who contributed to the full integration of Major League Baseball by franchises in both leagues.

1. Jackie Robinson played one year with the Kansas City Monarchs of the Negro Leagues before being signed to the Brooklyn Dodgers by Branch Rickey in 1945. Before his call up to the major leagues, Rickey had Robinson spend one year with this Canadian International League team in 1946, during which he won league MVP. What was the name of this minor league squad north of the border?

2. At what position did Robinson play all his games during his rookie season?

3. Toward the end of his stellar career, the Dodgers did the unthinkable and traded Robinson for pitcher Dick Littlefield and $30,000 in December 1956. Robinson chose to retire rather than continue his career with which franchise?

4. Two months after Robinson broke the color barrier, this player took the field in Cleveland as the first black American League player. A seven-time All-Star, he also became the first African-American HR leader and was a fixture on Cleveland's '48 and '54 WS teams. In 1954, he led the team in HR and RBI, and finished a near second to Yogi Berra in MVP voting. Who is this 1998 Cooperstown enshrinee?

5. The third black player to play in 1947 was this St. Louis Brown. Two days later, Willard Brown joined him on the Browns roster to become MLB's first pair of black teammates. In 1949, the pioneering Brown desegregated the New York Giants and was a fixture at third for the 1954 championship team, playing exceptionally during the series.

6. This Chicago White Sox barrier-breaker became only one of two men to play in five decades (1940s-80s, Nick Altrock the other). A seven-time All-Star, at age fifty he became the second-oldest man to appear in a major league game (after fifty-eight-year-old Satchel Paige). Name this well-aged, beloved White Sox.

7. This player actually appeared in the Giants lineup on the same day as the last man. After starring in the Negro, Mexican (he's enshrined in Mexico's Baseball Hall of Fame despite playing only 63 games), Puerto Rican and minor leagues, he finally broke into the majors at age thirty. Two seasons later, he led the NL in RBI and was third in MVP voting. His late-season brilliance thrust the Giants ahead in the 1951 pennant race that made Bobby Thomson's famous moment possible. In the World Series that followed, he had one of the greatest individual performances in postseason history. Name this great who was voted into Cooperstown in 1973.

8. So far, we've identified three players who became their franchise's first black player and were also voted into the Hall of Fame. A fourth man broke in as a twenty-two-year-old with the Cubs on September 17, 1953. Who was he?

9. In 1945, Jackie Robinson and this man were given an MLB tryout by none other than the late-to-integrate Red Sox. The great Hugh Duffy liked their skills, but neither was signed. Branch Rickey inked them instead but, worried about white fans' perception of the Dodgers having too many black players, later traded "The Jet" to Boston's NL outfit. Eventually, in 1950, this man won Rookie of the Year at age thirty-two, the oldest ever to win the award.

10. This first black Yankee was a ten-time All-Star and American League MVP in 1963. His many postseason appearances place him amongst or atop leaders in several World Series hitting and fielding categories. Traded to the Red Sox during their 1967 pennant drive, this man adeptly managed Boston's pitching staff to secure the Sox's first flag in more than twenty years. His number 32 is retired by the Yankees.

BLACK PIONEERS (ANSWERS)

1. Montreal Royals

2. First base

3. New York Giants

4. Larry Doby

5. Hank Thompson

6. Minnie Minoso

7. Monte Irvin

8. Ernie Banks

9. Sam Jethroe

10. Elston Howard

LONG AND LOYAL (1ST INNING)

These men deserve recognition for their longevity and loyalty. You are given the one team they played with their entire career, their position(s) and years played.

1. Baltimore Orioles 3B, 1955-1977

2. Boston Red Sox OF-1B, 1961-1983

3. Detroit Tigers OF, 1953-1974

4. St. Louis Cardinals OF-1B, 1941-1963

5. New York Giants OF, 1926-1947

6. Washington Senators P, 1907-1927

7. Pittsburgh Pirates OF-1B, 1962-1982

8. Chicago White Sox SS, 1930-1950

9. Cleveland Indians P, 1928-1947

10. Detroit Tigers 2B, 1924-1942

LONG AND LOYAL (1ST INNING ANSWERS)

1. Brooks Robinson

2. Carl Yastrzemski

3. Al Kaline

4. Stan Musial

5. Mel Ott

6. Walter Johnson

7. Willie Stargell

8. Luke Appling

9. Mel Harder

10. Charlie Gehringer

Fill in the Lineup (1st Inning)

Who's missing from these famous batting orders? Lineups are most frequent orders submitted by the manager for the chosen seasons.

1984 San Diego Padres

1. ? 2B
2. T Gwynn RF
3. ? 3B
4. S Garvey 1B
5. ? C
6. K McReynolds CF
7. C Martinez LF
8. ? SS
9. Pitcher

1927 New York Yankees

1. ? CF
2. M Koenig
3. ? RF
4. L Gehrig 1B
5. B Meusel LF
6. ? 2B
7. J Dugan 3B
8. P Collins C
9. Pitcher

1981 Montreal Expos

1. ? LF
2. R Scott 2B
3. ? CF
4. ? C
5. W Cromartie 1B
6. E Valentine RF
7. ? 3B
8. C Speier SS
9. Pitcher

1954 New York Giants

1. W Lockman 1B
2. ? SS
3. H Thompson 3B
4. ? LF
5. D Mueller RF
6. ? CF
7. D Williams 2B
8. W Westrum C
9. Pitcher

FILL IN THE LINEUP (1ST INNING ANSWERS)

1984 San Diego Padres
1. **Alan Wiggins 2B**
2. T Gwynn RF
3. **Craig Nettles 3B**
4. S Garvey 1B
5. **Terry Kennedy C**
6. K McReynolds CF
7. C Martinez LF
8. **Garry Templeton SS**
9. Pitcher

1927 New York Yankees
1. **Earl Combs CF**
2. M Koenig SS
3. **Babe Ruth RF**
4. L Gehrig 1B
5. B Meusel LF
6. **Tony Lazzeri 2B**
7. J Dugan 3B
8. P Collins C
9. Pitcher

1981 Montreal Expos
1. **Tim Raines LF**
2. R Scott 2B
3. **Andre Dawson CF**
4. **Gary Carter C**
5. W Cromartie 1B
6. E Valentine RF
7. **Larry Parrish 3B**
8. C Speier SS
9. Pitcher

1954 New York Giants
1. W Lockman 1B
2. **Al Dark SS**
3. H Thompson 3B
4. **Monte Irvin LF**
5. D Mueller RF
6. **Willie Mays CF**
7. D Williams 2B
8. W Westrum C
9. Pitcher

Ended Career with this Team (1st Inning)

Not every player is, or has the chance to be, loyal to one team for their entire career. The following players were popular for playing with one or more franchises. Oddity lies in the fact they ended their careers in some unusual places, certainly not where we identify them having their most productive seasons. Cases vary. Perhaps it's a player returning to a "home" state, an experienced hand added during a pennant chase or simply a faded veteran trying to hang on for one more year. In any case, it's meaningful trivia to know what uniform these particular players were wearing before hanging it up for good.

1. Harmon Killebrew

2. Larry Walker

3. Richie Ashburn

4. Dusty Baker

5. Yogi Berra

6. Wade Boggs

7. Jose Cruz

8. Luis Aparicio

9. Lou Boudreau

10. Dizzy Dean

ENDED CAREER WITH THIS TEAM (1ST INNING ANSWERS)

1. Kansas City Royals (1975)

2. St. Louis Cardinals (2005)

3. New York Mets (1962)

4. Oakland A's (1986)

5. New York Mets (1965)

6. Tampa Bay Devil Rays (1999)

7. New York Yankees (1988)

8. Boston Red Sox (1973)

9. Boston Red Sox (1952)

10. St. Louis Browns (1947)

Most Home Runs by Two Teammates

Each pair of these teammates combined for at least 600 home runs while playing on the same roster. You are given the team, years they played together, and their combined and individual HR totals. Name these potent pairs:

1. Boston (NL), Milwaukee, 1954-66: 442 + 421 = 863

2. San Francisco Giants, 1959-71: 430 + 370 = 800

3. Boston Red Sox, 1974-89: 382 + 355 = 737

4. Brooklyn/Los Angeles Dodgers, 1947-61: 384 + 361 = 745

5. New York Yankees, 1923-34: 511 + 348 = 859

6. Chicago Cubs, 1960-73: 376 + 337 = 713

7. Houston Astros, 1991-2005: 449 + 240 = 689

8. Texas Rangers, 1989-2003: 372 + 321 = 693

9. Oakland A's, 1986-92, 1997: 363 + 249 = 612

10. New York Yankees, 1951-63: 419 + 283 = 702

11. Seattle Mariners, 1989-99: 398 + 269 = 667

12. Atlanta Braves, 1996-2007: 368 + 363 = 731

MOST HOME RUNS BY TWO TEAMMATES (ANSWERS)

1. Hank Aaron and Eddie Matthews

2. Willie Mays and Willie McCovey

3. Jim Rice and Dwight Evans

4. Duke Snider and Gil Hodges

5. Babe Ruth and Lou Gehrig

6. Billy Williams and Ron Santo

7. Jeff Bagwell and Craig Biggio

8. Juan Gonzalez and Rafael Palmeiro

9. Mark McGwire and Jose Canseco

10. Mickey Mantle and Yogi Berra

11. Ken Griffey Jr. and Jay Buhner

12. Andruw Jones and Chipper Jones

Hall of Famer Anagrams

The following phrases are actually a reshuffling of the letters contained in the name of a baseball Hall of Famer. Rearrange them to reveal these legendary lettermen.

1. Long Relief Sir, Ring For Leslie, Iron Fig Seller, Rise Long Rifle

2. Falcon Skirt, Fort Calkins, Sick Frontal, Calfskin Rot, Fat Corn Silk

3. Uglier Hog, Oh I Gurgle, I Rule Gogh, Hugo Rigel

4. Joe Ginger Sack, Sign Eager Jock, Gas Joke Cringe, Jocks in Reggae

5. Rhino Embark Well, Beer Hill Workmen, Roar Nimble Whelk

6. Anger By Nerds, Synge Bernard, Render By Snag, Snag End Berry

7. We Rear Veal, A Revere Law, We're Larvae, Reveal Wear

8. Fan A Dusky Ox, Found A Sky Ax, Yukon Sax Fad, Day Of Sunk Ax

9. Fade Evil Wind, A Dwindle Five, Field And View

10. Sheen Didn't Score, Scorn Dense Edith, Enter Second Dish, Sirs Encoded Then

HALL OF FAMER ANAGRAMS (ANSWERS)

1. Rollie Fingers

2. Carlton Fisk

3. Lou Gehrig

4. Reggie Jackson

5. Harmon Killebrew

6. Ryne Sandberg

7. Earl Weaver

8. Sandy Koufax

9. Dave Winfield

10. Red Schoendienst

MICKEY MANTLE ★★★ Played 1951–1968

CAREER STATISTICS

Mickey Charles Mantle, who played centerfield for the New York Yankees for 18 years, is sixteenth on the list of all-time home runs. He hit 536 and never fewer than the 13 home runs he hit in his rookie year. Mantle compiled ten years of an average of .300 or higher, retiring with a lifetime average of .298. He played in 12 World Series, hitting 18 home runs while helping the Yankees

Batting average	.298
At bats	8,102
Hits	2,414
Doubles	344
Home runs	536
Runs scored	1,677
Runs batted in	1,509
Bases on balls	1,734

win seven Series. Mantle was inducted into the Baseball Hall of Fame in 1974.

Mickey Mantle was born on October 20, 1931 in Spavinaw, Oklahoma. His father, Elvin "Mutt" Mantle, was a huge baseball fan and named his firstborn son after Mickey Cochrane, the Hall of Fame catcher. (Mickey always said he was lucky his father never knew Mickey Cochrane's real name was Gordon Stanley Cochrane.) Mutt Mantle was a lead miner who once played semipro ball. He intended for his son Mickey to achieve everything he couldn't. Mickey spent his childhood playing baseball and being coached by his father. He started switch-hitting as soon as he was swinging the bat (his natural side was right-handed).

Mantle joined the Yankee outfield in 1951, playing in right field alongside the legendary Joe DiMaggio. When a ball hit by rookie Willie Mays came between Mantle and DiMaggio in right-centerfield tragedy struck. Joltin' Joe caught the ball but Mickey, in full sprint, stepped on a drainage cover with his cleats and tore the cartilage in his right knee. Mantle would never again play pain-free but he did play extraordinarily well–in 1956 he won the Triple Crown and MVP award

In an exhibition game at the University of Southern California during his rookie spring training season that year, batting left-handed, he hit a home run ball that left the ball field and crossed an adjacent football field, traveling an estimated 656 feet.

with 52 home runs, a .353 batting average, and 130 RBIs.

THE SLUGGERS

WORLD SERIES STATS

The Yankees monopolize many records amassed in World Series play, as you might guess. You'll come across some pinstripes in the following queries, along with an ample amount of postseason stars from other winning teams. Name these men who gave their best performances when it mattered most.

1. After some bootleg postseason performances early in his career, this man blew up in the 2002 World Series to record a 1.294 slugging average in 30 plate appearances.

2. Whose 10 wins in World Series play is an all-time record? Need we say he was a Yankee?

3. Mickey Mantle could be the answer to a slew of questions in this category, including most WS runs, HRs and RBI, but a teammate of his has the distinction of appearing in the most (75) WS games – ten more than The Mick.

4. Two Hall of Famers share the record for most Series stolen bases with fourteen. One snatched seven in both the 1967 and '68 Fall Classics, the same sum that an Athletics/White Sox second baseman steadily stole over six Series in the 1910s.

5. In the 1990 WS, this red-hot Red hatcheted A's pitching for 9 hits in 12 at-bats. His .750 average is a single-Series record, and, if you're not fussy about plate appearances, a career record, too.

6. Hey, guy – remember a few decades back when that guy hit five dongs against Los Angeles in the Series? Well, turns out some Philly infielder just tied his record like two years ago. Huh? I don't know their names. That's why I'm askin' you!

7. This cog in the Big Red Machine rotation posted an amazing 0.36 ERA in more than three Series. Got billed for only one run in 25.1 innings. Not surprising considering Christy Mathewson was his cousin...

8. Speaking of Mathewson, his three WS shutouts in 1905 set a scoreless innings record – but it's a shared record. In 1921, a HOF Yankee also posted a 0.00 ERA over 27 WS frames. However, after victories in Games 2 and 5, the Giants bested him 1-0 on a run-scoring error in the deciding game of the Series.

9. In four Series with the Yankees and one with the White Sox, this pitcher established a career record for strikeouts per 9 innings at 11.30 Ks in 29 frames.

10. Let's go to the set-up man before bringing in the closer. Interestingly, both the set-up man and closer we're referring to played for the 1996 World Series Champion Yankees and each holds a Series saves record. However, the set-up man has more saves than the closer. The record for most saves in a World Series by a closer was set when the closer with more World Series saves set him up to close. For the record, this is closer to giving away the answer than we set-up for, so to be safe we'll save the part about who's closer to most saves in a World Series than the closer who saved the most World Series games. You must be close to an answer by now.

WORLD SERIES STATS (ANSWERS)

1. Barry Bonds

2. Whitey Ford

3. Yogi Berra

4. Lou Brock and Eddie Collins

5. Billy Hatcher

6. Reggie Jackson and Chase Utley

7. Jack Billingham

8. Waite Hoyt

9. Orlando Hernandez

10. Mariano Rivera (11 career WS saves) and John Wetteland (4 saves in '96)

THEY BECAME THEM

Each of these franchises either picked up and moved to a different city or changed their names while remaining in the same city. Name the team they're known as today.

1. Montreal Expos

2. St. Louis Browns

3. Houston Colt .45s

4. Washington Senators (1960)

5. Washington Senators (repackaged for 1961 and again shipped out of capital a decade later)

6. Seattle Pilots (this team was in port for only one year, 1969, before sailing east)

7. 1902 Baltimore Orioles

8. 1902 Chicago Orphans

9. This team wavered back and forth on a long list of nicknames, including the "Bridegrooms," "Superbas" and "Robins" before settling on a name they carry today after being transplanted to the West Coast in 1957.

10. This team, whose name has been used for the longest period in American sports history, were not without a few attempts by ownership to change their moniker. As part of a name-changing contest held by team owner Robert Carpenter, this team was called the Blue Jays for two years, 1943 and '44.

THEY BECAME THEM (ANSWERS)

1. Washington Nationals

2. Baltimore Orioles

3. Houston Astros

4. Minnesota Twins

5. Texas Rangers

6. Milwaukee Brewers

7. New York Highlanders. Changed name to Yankees a few years later.

8. Chicago Cubs

9. Los Angeles Dodgers

10. Philadelphia Phillies

HALL OF FAMERS ON SAME TEAM

Each of the following memorable teams featured at least four Hall of Famers in their dugout, managers included. The total number of HOFers is in parentheses. Identify as many you can – and consider yourself correct if you can guess a majority of the names.

1. 1975 Cincinnati Reds (4)

2. 1955 Brooklyn Dodgers (7)

3. 1956 New York Yankees (6)

4. 1978 New York Yankees (4)

5. 1938 Boston Red Sox (5)

6. 1983 Philadelphia Phillies (4)

7. 1970 Chicago Cubs (5)

8. 1928 Philadelphia A's (8)

9. 1972 Oakland A's (5)

10. 1978 San Diego Padres (4)

11. 1964 San Francisco Giants (6)

12. 1933 St. Louis Cardinals (8)

HALL OF FAMERS ON SAME TEAM (ANSWERS)

1. Johnny Bench, Joe Morgan, Tony Perez, Manager Sparky Anderson

2. Roy Campanella, Tommy Lasorda, Pee Wee Reese, Jackie Robinson, Duke Snider, Dick Williams, Manager Walter Alston

3. Yogi Berra, Whitey Ford, Mickey Mantle, Phil Rizzuto, Enos Slaughter, Manager Casey Stengel

4. Rich Gossage, Catfish Hunter, Reggie Jackson, Manager Bob Lemon

5. Bobby Doerr, Jimmie Foxx, Lefty Grove, Ted Williams, Player/Manager Joe Cronin

6. Steve Carlton, Joe Morgan, Tony Perez, Mike Schmidt

7. Ernie Banks, Ferguson Jenkins, Hoyt Wilhelm, Billy Williams, Manager Leo Durocher

8. Ty Cobb, Mickey Cochrane, Eddie Collins, Jimmie Foxx, Lefty Grove, Al Simmons, Tris Speaker, Manager Connie Mack

9. Orlando Cepeda, Rollie Fingers, Catfish Hunter, Reggie Jackson, Manager Dick Williams

10. Rollie Fingers, Gaylord Perry, Ozzie Smith, Dave Winfield

11. Orlando Cepeda, Juan Marichal, Willie Mays, Willie McCovey, Gaylord Perry, Duke Snider

12. Dizzy Dean, Leo Durocher, Burleigh Grimes, Jesse Haines, Rogers Hornsby, Joe Medwick, Dazzy Vance, Player/Manager Frankie Frisch

NICKNAMES (1ST INNING)

Each of the following is a Hall of Famer with a famous nickname. Identify these players' actual names.

1. The Splendid Splinter

2. The Yankee Clipper

3. The Wizard of Oz

4. Charlie Hustle

5. Kung-Fu Panda

6. Say Hey Kid

7. The Silver Fox

8. The Commerce Comet

9. The Georgia Peach

10. Louisiana Lightning

11. Big Poison

12. The Toy Cannon

Nicknames (1st Inning answers)

1. Ted Williams

2. Joe DiMaggio

3. Ozzie Smith

4. Pete Rose

5. Pablo Sandoval

6. Willie Mays

7. Duke Snider

8. Mickey Mantle

9. Ty Cobb

10. Ron Guidry

11. Paul Waner

12. Jimmy Wynn

HARMON KILLEBREW ★★★ Played 1954–1975

Harmon Clayton "Killer" Killebrew had eight seasons in which he hit over 40 home runs. He led the American League in home runs six times and in RBIs three times. With 573 home runs in his career, he is eleventh on the all-time list. Killebrew was inducted into the Baseball Hall of Fame in 1984.

CAREER STATISTICS

Batting average	.256
At bats	8,147
Hits	2,086
Doubles	290
Home runs	573
Runs scored	1,283
Runs batted in	1,584
Bases on balls	1,559

Harmon Killebrew did not hit for a high average but he packed plenty of power. For 14 consecutive seasons, he hit more than 20 home runs, and in eight of those seasons, he hit more than 40. He drew numerous free passes, leading the American League four times in bases on balls with 103 in 1966, 131 in 1967, 145 in 1969 and 114 in 1971. In 1969, when he led the league in four offensive categories, including 49 home runs, he was voted the year's MVP.

The early going of his career was hardly indicative of a player who was headed to Cooperstown. When Killebrew signed his professional contract with the Washington Senators, major league baseball's "bonus rule" required that a player who signed for more than a $4,000 bonus had to be kept on the major league roster for two years. As a "bonus" player, he didn't see much action in 1954 and 1955 (his first two years), playing a total of only 47 major league games. After three years in the minors, Killebrew returned to the Senators, blasting 42 home runs and driving in 105 runs. His career, which landed Killer in the Baseball Hall of Fame, was off and running.

Killebrew was given the nickname "Killer" because he tried to murder the ball every time he swung the bat. He never got cheated on a swing, putting his entire body into it. Even though he struck out 1,699 times, Killebrew will always be better remembered for his long, towering home runs. As a dependable run producer, Killer eschewed the sacrifice bunt—he never had one in his career, in which he racked up 8,147 at bats.

In his only trip to the World Series—in 1965 when Killebrew and the Twins met and lost to the Los Angeles Dodgers—he banged out six hits, including a solo home run against Dodger pitcher Don Drysdale.

THE SLUGGERS

WHERE ARE WE?

AYU space-time engineers have developed a time machine in the form of a bullpen buggy. Let's punch in some dates and visit some "moments" in baseball history. Your job as co-pilot is to identify the city, town or ballpark we find ourselves in.

1. We're in the right field grandstand of this stadium waiting for the start of Game 3 of the 1989 World Series, when suddenly a 7.1 magnitude earthquake has the stands rippling like waves. The quake delayed the Series for several days and caused catastrophic damage to the Bay Area.

2. It's 1930 and somehow I'm catching, and you're at the plate, batting lefty with a pond full of Brooklyn Robins (looks like Sloppy Thurston at third, Val Picinich at second, Del Bissonette at first). You're choked up on your bat like an ungainly Mel Ott, looking to pull a grand slam around the short pole in right, only 257 feet away. I say: show some Depression Era sack and go for straightaway center, more than 500 feet deep. Just then I get crossed up on a drooling spitter from Fat Freddie Fitzsimmons and am sprinting seventy feet to the backstop to retrieve a passed ball!

3. We've got box seats for Game 3 of the 1932 World Series. Babe Ruth steps to the plate amid a cacophony of mocking from the home team dugout. Ruth barbs back and seemingly levels his arm, gesturing at the outfield seats. Ruth then knocks Charlie Root's next pitch toward center and the ball clears the wall for a homer. Did he just call his own round-tripper? Coming around third, Ruth is gesturing emphatically at the dugout as if the hit was an answer to the insults levied upon him by what opposing team?

4. It's October 4, 1971, Game 4 of the World Series, and we're in the third tier of this stadium's left field under a glowing grid of lights watching the first night game in Fall Classic history.

5. It's June 19, 1846, and we're standing amongst a human warning track in the outfield watching baseball's first officially organized game, at Elysian Fields in this city. The Knickerbocker Base Ball Club is losing badly after the New York Nine scores 21 runs for a game-ending "ace." With last ups,

the Knicks fail to answer and umpire Alexander Cartwright calls the game. Final official score: New York Nine 23, Knickerbockers 1.

6. It's 1934, and we're in the stands watching a fifteen-year-old kid named Ted Williams corkscrew his skinny frame into long hits for Herbert Hoover High School in this city.

7. It's 4:07 a.m. on April 18, 1981, and an usher has poked us both awake to tell us that the AAA game we started watching the day before has been suspended after 32 innings of 2-2 deadlocked ball. The usher didn't mention it was the longest game in pro baseball history, but did say the game would resume later that night. When a second Rhode Island moon appears over the same contest, Marty Barrett scores in the bottom of the 33rd inning to win the marathon game for what minor league squad?

8. It's July 17, 1961, and we're at the deathbed of the legendary Ty Cobb at Emory University Hospital in this city. On the bedstand is a loaded gun and stack of paper bonds with a face amount of $1 million, representing the wealth he amassed from investments in a fledgling local company some years before. Extra points if you can guess what he invested in.

9. All this time travel has made us thirsty. How about a drink at the Cask 'n Flagon on the corner of Brookline and Lansdowne behind this ballpark?

10. It's 1839, and we're standing in the middle of a cow pasture, the property of Mr. Elihu Phinney. We're waiting for U.S. Military Cadet and future Civil War General Abner Doubleday to show up and invent baseball. Contrary to history, he never shows, leaving us ankle-deep in cow pies.

11. The Orioles plate a run in the top of the 11th to win 3-2 in a 1999 exhibition game against this nation's national side, their first contest against a major league team in forty years.

WHERE ARE WE? (ANSWERS)

1. San Francisco, CA (Candlestick Park)

2. Upper Manhattan, NYC (Polo Grounds)

3. Chicago, IL (Wrigley Field)

4. Pittsburgh, PA (Three Rivers Stadium)

5. Hoboken, NJ

6. San Diego, CA

7. Pawtucket Red Sox (McCoy Stadium)

8. Atlanta, GA (Cobb had invested in Coca-Cola)

9. Fenway Park

10. Cooperstown, NY

11. Havana, Cuba

MISCELLANEOUS MILESTONES (1ST INNING)

Appropriate the following questions into your trivia portfolio.

1. Perhaps 643 would have been a more suitable uniform number than 14 for this Red Sox slugger, who in 1984 grounded into a season-record 36 double plays.

2. In 1971, this masochistic Expo infielder left a mark in record books when he was hit by 50 pitches, the most in a single season during the modern era.

3. Before Barry Bonds' unreasonable allowance of free passes, another Giant held the record for intentional base-on-balls when, in 1969, obsequious opponents opted to walk him 45 times.

4. Manny Mota's long-standing record of 150 pinch hits has been topped twice in the new century. This eighteen-year vet of service with eight NL teams holds the new mark with 212 hits, amassed over another record 804 pinch-hit at-bats from 1988-2005.

5. Can you name the lefty-throwing, righty-batting pitcher who holds the record for Silver Slugger Awards won by a hurler? He won five in a row from 1999-2003, a stretch in which he played with four different clubs.

6. The record for outfield assists in a season – 44 – was set by this Phillie great in 1930. Playing a shallow right in the new Baker Bowl allowed him to gun down many hitters at first base on would-be singles.

7. This kid blew into the league with a rookie record of 115 stolen bases in 1985 en route to the Rookie of the Year Award. He proved a copycat the next two years, a record for consecutive 100-plus SB seasons.

8. The first modern era player to steal 100 bases did it with the 1962 Dodgers, which accelerated the motion to declare him MVP that year.

MISCELLANEOUS MILESTONES (1ST INNING ANSWERS)

1. Jim Rice

2. Ron Hunt

3. Willie McCovey

4. Lenny Harris

5. Mike Hampton

6. Chuck Klein

7. Vince Coleman

8. Maury Wills

NAME'S THE SAME (1ST INNING)

The following groups of people all have a name in common. Name that name.

1. Lance, Larry, John

2. Bob, Chet, Jim

3. Ken, Dave, Rickey

4. Glenn, Jody, Storm

5. Alex, Ban, Charles

6. Damian, Stu, Huggins

7. Adams, Herman, Dahlgren

8. Curt, Ted, Al

9. Billy, Darrell, Dwight

10. Roy, Devon, Rondell

11. Grimsley, Gload, Youngs

12. Eddie, Jimmy, Ripper, Shano

Name's the Same (1st Inning answers)

1. Parrish

2. Lemon

3. Henderson

4. Davis

5. Johnson

6. Miller

7. Babe

8. Simmons

9. Evans

10. White

11. Ross

12. Collins

REGGIE JACKSON ★★★ Played 1967–1987

CAREER STATISTICS

Reginald Martinez "Mr. October" Jackson is thirteenth on the all-time list of home run leaders. He played in five World Series, compiling a .357 batting average. In Series play he is sixth in slugging percentage (.755), fifth in home runs (10) and eighth in RBIs (24). Jackson was inducted into the Baseball Hall of Fame in 1993.

Batting average	.262
At bats	9,864
Hits	2,584
Doubles	463
Home runs	563
Runs scored	1,551
Runs batted in	1,702
Bases on balls	1,375

Reggie Jackson was born in Wyncote, Pennsylvania, in 1946. His father had been a player in the Negro Leagues. In high school it looked as though Jackson might use his athletic talent elsewhere. Even though he was an outstanding baseball player, it was football that brought him all the early attention. He was offered an amazing 51 scholarships from various colleges.

Jackson chose Arizona State, where he played football and baseball. The Kansas City Athletics signed Jackson and in 1968, when the team moved to Oakland, he hit 29 home runs. In 1969, he slammed 47 home runs to validate his standing as a slugging run producer (he had 118 RBIs as well in 1969). Remarkably, he accomplished this while leading the league in strikeouts (142)–the second of four consecutive years of this dubious honor. Jackson is first on the career strikeout list with 2,597.

For 16 of his 21 playing years Jackson hit more than 20 home runs, including five years in which he slammed more than 30 homes runs and two 40-plus home run years. He belted a league-leading 41 home runs in 1980, when as a New York Yankee under the tutelage of legendary hitting coach Charley Lau he batted .300, his only season batting .300 or better.

Jackson came to the Yankees in 1977 after being traded to Baltimore for a single season. Jackson and New York were a great combination. Jackson once said, "If I ever played in New York, they'd name a candy bar after me." They did.

Jackson led the Yankees to two World Series championships, in 1977 and 1978. In the 1977 Series, he batted .450 and hit five home runs, and in 1978, he hit .397 and hit two home runs. His World Series performances earned him the nickname, "Mr. October."

THE SLUGGERS

TEAMMATES WHO FINISHED 1ST & 2ND IN AWARD VOTING

The following teammates finished one-two in MVP, Cy Young or Rookie of the Year voting. Name these winners and near winners.

1. Roger Maris edged out teammate Mickey Mantle for AL MVP in both 1960 and '61. In each case, Mantle lost by .01 percentage points. The Mick finally captured the award in '62, not beating out Maris, but this light-hitting second baseman teammate who will always be remembered for his leaping, World Series-ending snag of a Willie McCovey liner in the bottom of the 9th in Game 7 of the '62 Fall Classic.

2. This Diamondback pitching duo finished one-two for the Cy Young in 2001 and 2002. The same man won the award both times (and again in 2003), but luckily they got to share the World Series MVP in 2001.

3. These top two Giant vote getters in the 2000 MVP balloting couldn't stand each other, which was fine for all the folks who couldn't stand either of them. The second baseman won it over the outfielder by posting a batting average .027 points higher (.334) and driving in 19 more runs (125 RBI) than his pal who was still able to collect seven of the trophies over his career anyway.

4. It's hard to decide which of these guys was the more petulant Pirate – 1990 MVP Gold Glove left fielder or that year's MVP runner-up right fielder. It's worth noting the right fielder, a six-time All-Star, started out for the Pirates in 1987 as a third baseman but was moved to the outfield after committing 67 errors at the hot corner in 1988 and '89. Both of these players have sub-.250 batting averages for their postseason careers.

5. Nicknamed the "Golddust Twins," this outfield duo helped the Red Sox win the AL pennant in 1975. The center fielder ran away with the ROY and MVP awards that year, with a Gold Glove to boot. The left fielder was number two in ROY voting and finished third in MVP voting. In the end, the left fielder is a HOF candidate with a strong lobby while the center fielder will have to be satisfied with enshrinement in the Red Sox and College Baseball halls of fame.

6. The Giants packed a one-two punch when these teammates finished at the top of the MVP voting in 1989, the same year they lost to the A's in the earthquake-marred, Bay Bridge World Series. Despite a career with nine teams, his '89 season is worthy of attention considering the left fielder belted 47 HRs, drove in 125 runs and hit .291. His sweet-swinging

second-place teammate, who played at Mississippi State with Bobby Thigpen and Rafael Palmeiro, had a steadier career at first base.

7. It's not surprising the 1966 Baltimore Orioles won 97 games and swept the World Series when you consider their right fielder, third baseman and first baseman finished one-two-three in the MVP voting that year. The right fielder not only won the MVP, but also the Triple Crown by hitting .316 with 49 HRs and 122 RBI – and the WS MVP to boot. The slick-fielding third sacker won his own MVP in '64, and the thickset first sacker took the trophy in 1970. In 1966, these 3-4-5 hitters (in batting order) combined for 106 regular season HRs.

8. These Pirate teammates finished one-two in the MVP balloting in 1960 and went on to win the World Series over two Yankee teammates who accomplished the same one-two feat that season. The MVP SS was a former Duke point guard and five-time All-Star who led the league with a .325 average in '60. He beat out his third baseman teammate, a man who died tragically at forty-one from a heart attack suffered at the wheel of his car. Despite accomplished seasons, neither player hit over .220 in the 1960 WS. The shared "oa" diphthong in both players' monosyllabic last names sounds especially good in a Pittsburgh accent.

9. In 1971, an A's pitcher finished first in the MVP balloting and a teammate finished second. The staff ace, only twenty-one, started the All-Star Game and won the Cy Young that year. The third baseman/captain held the team together while hitting .291 with 24 HRs and 94 RBI. Their seasons were only enough to get them to the ALCS, where the Orioles swept them. But these two men continued to play important roles on an A's dynasty that won World Series the following three years.

10. The 1965 Twins came out of nowhere to take the AL pennant with an array of teammates contributing to their success. Not surprisingly, the top two MVP vote getters in the AL were the great-gloving, light-hitting SS and excellent-hitting RF on that team. The SS received all but one first-place vote from writers. Who is he and which of his teammates (ROY the season prior) got that one other vote?

TEAMMATES WHO FINISHED 1ST & 2ND IN AWARD VOTING (ANSWERS)

1. Bobby Richardson

2. Randy Johnson and Curt Schilling

3. Jeff Kent and Barry Bonds

4. Barry Bonds and Bobby Bonilla

5. Fred Lynn and Jim Rice

6. Kevin Mitchell and Will Clark

7. Frank Robinson, Brooks Robinson and Boog Powell

8. Dick Groat and Don Hoak

9. Vida Blue and Sal Bando

10. Zoilo Versalles and Tony Oliva

MIKE SCHMIDT ★★★ Played 1972–1989

CAREER STATISTICS

Batting average	.267
At bats	8,352
Hits	2,234
Doubles	408
Home runs	548
Runs scored	1,506
Runs batted in	1,595
Bases on balls	1,507

Michael Jack Schmidt was the Philadelphia Phillies third baseman for 18 years. He is fifteenth on the all-time list for home runs, with 548. He won eight home run titles, the most ever for a National League player. For 14 consecutive seasons, he hit more than 20 home runs, and with the exception of 1978, he hit more than 30. Schmidt, who won three MVP awards, was inducted into the Baseball Hall of Fame in 1995.

Mike Schmidt was born on September 27, 1949 in Dayton, Ohio. He loved baseball as a youth but struggled to excel in his favorite sport. Overcoming operations on his knees, and disregarding advice that he give up sports, he persevered. Although he never won a single baseball award during his high school years, his play in college at Ohio University attracted the attention of major league scouts. And in 1971 he was selected in the second round of the amateur draft.

In his rookie season in 1973, Schmidt managed to hit 18 home runs despite a batting average of .196. He followed up this inauspicious start with three consecutive years of tremendous slugging–hitting league-leading totals of 36, 38 and 38 home runs respectively. He also led the National League those years in RBI with 116, 95 and 107.

In 1976 Schmidt hit four home runs in a game against the Chicago Cubs at Wrigley Field. Down 12-1 after three innings, the Phillies rallied. Schmidt hit a home run in the fifth with a man on, then in the seventh he smacked another home run.

Mike Schmidt hit one of the longest singles ever. In the Houston Astrodome Schmidt hit a towering drive that struck a speaker in centerfield. The ball dropped to the field–in play, according to the ground rules–and Schmidt had to stop at first base with a single.

The score was now 13-7. The comeback had begun. In the eighth inning, Schmidt belted his third home run, this time with two men on base, bringing the Phillies to within one run, 13-12. The teams tied after nine innings at 15-15 and in the tenth, Schmidt slugged his fourth home run of the game. The final score: Phillies 18, Cubs 16.

THE SLUGGERS

BASEBALL LINEAGES: RED SOX LEFT FIELDERS

Left field had long been a position of renown for the Boston Red Sox. Not only does the great Green Monster pose one of the most peculiar conundrums in fielding batted balls, but it has also been the backdrop to a select group of Red Sox legends spanning the full century of Fenway Park's existence. Name the missing men in this timeline of Monster Minders.

BOSTON RED SOX LEFT FIELDERS			
YEARS	PLAYER	YEARS	PLAYER
		1939-42	
1912-17	1.?	1943	Johnny Lazor
		1944-45	Bob Johnson
1918-19	2.?	1946-51	3.?
1920-22	Mike Menosky		
		1952-53	Hoot Evers
1923-37	11 Players	1954-60	
1938-39	Joe Vosmik		

BOSTON RED SOX LEFT FIELDERS			
YEARS	PLAYER	YEARS	PLAYER
1961-72	4.?	1988-96	6.?
		1997	Wil Cordero
1973-74	Tommy Harper	1998-2001	7.?
1975-87	5.?	2002-08	8.?
		2009	Jason Bay
		2010	Daniel Nava
		2011	ugh...

BASEBALL LINEAGES: RED SOX LEFT FIELDERS (ANSWERS)

1. Duffy Lewis

2. Babe Ruth

3. Ted Williams

4. Carl Yastrzemski

5. Jim Rice

6. Mike Greenwell

7. Troy O'Leary

8. Manny Ramirez

REAL FIRST NAMES

Can you guess the first name these players have listed on their birth certificate?

1. Chipper Jones

2. Satchel Paige

3. Cy Young

4. Bo Jackson

5. Pee Wee Reese

6. Whitey Ford

7. Dizzy Dean

8. Lefty Gomez

9. Tris Speaker

10. Al Simmons

11. Nap Lajoie

12. Ken Griffey Jr.

REAL FIRST NAMES (ANSWERS)

1. Larry

2. Leroy

3. Denton

4. Vincent

5. Harold

6. Edward

7. Jay

8. Vernon

9. Tristram

10. Aloysius

11. Napoleon

12. George

MORE RBI THAN GAMES PLAYED

Each of these players accomplished an impressive feat: knocking in an average of more than one run per game in a season with at least 100 games played. Name them.

1. This RBI king played in only 155 games in 1930 yet hacked in 36 more RBI than that number.

2. This Yankee legend had more RBI than games played in four separate seasons, including an amazing 167/151 season in 1937.

3. In 1949, these two Red Sox each rapped out 159 RBI in 155 games.

4. In 1950, this 6-foot-5 Red Sox had 144 RBI in only 136 games played in his Rookie of the Year season. He broke his wrist the next season and never again had more than 100 RBI.

5. In 1931, this Yankee set the AL record for differential between RBI and games played with a gap of twenty-nine. His season mark of 184 RBI remains a Junior Circuit record.

6. In 1937, this heavy-hitting Tiger tied that mark of twenty-nine. He was one off in tying the last man's season RBI total with only 183 that year.

7. In 1980, this Royal played in only 117 games but finished the season with one more RBI than that number.

8. In 1998, this slugger rapped out 157 RBI in 154 games. He and Hank Greenberg are the only players ever to have at least 100 RBI by the All-Star Break.

9. In 1999, this ditzy Cleveland left fielder had 165 RBI in 147 games.

10. In 1936, this Indian had 162 RBI in 151 games, beating out league MVP Lou Gehrig that season for the lead in RBI, extra-base hits and total bases.

MORE RBI THAN GAMES PLAYED (ANSWERS)

1. Hack Wilson

2. Joe DiMaggio

3. Ted Williams and Vern Stephens

4. Walt Dropo

5. Lou Gehrig

6. Hank Greenberg

7. George Brett

8. Juan Gonzalez

9. Manny Ramirez

10. Hal Trosky

BATTERY MATES (1ST INNING)

Identify the greater pitchers by their battery mates. We limited clues to their most frequent backstops, with a few catchers of note tagged on as well. (GC–Games caught for respective pitcher)

1.	CATCHER	GC		2.	Catcher	GC
	Alan Ashby	136			Tim McCarver	228
	Terry Humphrey	65			Bob Boone	146
	Jerry Grote	57			Bo Diaz	79
	Craig Biggio	9			Ted Simmons	46

3.				4.		
	Tim McCarver	197			Randy Hundley	188
	Ted Simmons	135			Jim Sundberg	175
	Joe Torre	22			Jody Davis	54
	Bob Uecker	16			Carlton Fisk	49

5.				6.		
	Johnny Roseboro	208			Yogi Berra	212
	Jeff Torborg	21			Elston Howard	179
	Roy Campanella	18			Johnny Blanchard	25

7.				8.		
	Joe Girardi	85			Mickey Cochrane	224
	Gary Carter	52			Gene Desautels	82
	Mackey Sasser	42			Rick Ferrell	64
	Mike Macfarlane	37			Jimmie Foxx	7

9.				10.		
	Jason Varitek	106			Eddie Perez	121
	Darren Daulton	97			Henry Blanco	82
	Mike Lieberthal	94			Damon Berryhill	81
	Damian Miller	71			Joe Girardi	48
	Craig Biggio	46			Jody Davis	45

11.				12.		
	Tom Haller	125			Chief Myers	186
	Dick Dietz	94			Frank Bowerman	133
	Ed Bailey	62			Roger Bresnahan	97

BATTERY MATES (1ST INNING ANSWERS)

	PITCHER	CAREER STARTS
1.	Nolan Ryan	773
2.	Steve Carlton	709
3.	Bob Gibson	482
4.	Ferguson Jenkins	594
5.	Sandy Koufax	313
6.	Whitey Ford	438
7.	David Cone	419
8.	Lefty Grove	457
9.	Curt Schilling	436
10.	Greg Maddux	740
11.	Juan Marichal	457
12.	Christy Mathewson	552

BASEBALL LITERATURE

Answer the following questions related to baseball as a literary subject.

1. What once-ostracized pitcher wrote an exposé on the Yankees clubhouse called *Ball Four*?

2. What spacey lefty's autobiography is titled *The Wrong Stuff*?

3. *The Boys of Summer* is a memoir about what baseball team?

4. What word did Bill Veeck use in the title of his memoir as a clue to the pronunciation of his name?

5. Whose autobiography is titled *I Had A Hammer*?

6. David Halberstam's *The Teammates* recounts the elderly friendship between four players from what American League team?

7. What fiction team does Roy Hobbs play for in Bernard Malamud's *The Natural*?

8. Who is the subject of Nicholas Dawidoff's *The Catcher Was a Spy*?

9. John Updike's "Hub Fans Bid Kid Adieu" is an essay on a city's goodbye to what Hall of Famer?

10. Name the team and season studied in Eliot Asinof's *Eight Men Out*.

11. What two men reached base before Casey came to bat in Ernest Thayer's *Casey at the Bat*?

12. Robert DeNiro starred as fated catcher Bruce Pearson in what movie version of a Mark Harris novel?

BASEBALL LITERATURE (ANSWERS)

1. Jim Bouton

2. Bill Lee

3. The Brooklyn Dodgers

4. Wreck (Veeck as in Wreck)

5. Hank Aaron

6. Boston Red Sox

7. New York Knights

8. Moe Berg

9. Ted Williams

10. 1919 Chicago White Sox

11. "Flynn" and "(Jimmy) Blake"

12. "Bang the Drum Slowly"

GOLD GLOVE FIRST BASEMEN

The following men each won at least three Gold Gloves at first base. Notable facts about each player are included in the questions.

1. This Cub won four Gold Glove awards and was no slouch at the plate either – he led all of MLB in hits during the 1990s.
2. This 1979 co-MVP holds the record for most GGs won at first with eleven.
3. "Boomer" won a total of eight GGs with the Red Sox and Brewers in the '60s and '70s.
4. From 1958-64, this Puerto Rican-born player won every AL GG at first base, playing with the A's, Indians and Twins. The powerful name we know him by is an Americanized one, but his birth certificate reads Victor Felipe Pellot Pove.
5. This slick fielder had good hands in his genes. His father was a receiver at Notre Dame and had an eleven-year NFL career with the Rams. The son won six straight GGs from 1995-2000 – two with the Angels and four with the Giants.
6. This Cardinal won seven straight GGs from 1960-66. He was a fixture on the 1964 World Series Championship team and later became National League President from 1989-94.
7. "Mr. Steady" played only nine seasons with the Los Angeles Dodgers, but collected six GGs in that time. Amongst all the great fielders at first base in the fifty-year span of Rawlings' award, fans chose this man as the first baseman on the All-Time Gold Glove team in 2007.
8. Plagued by back problems that cut short a prolific career, this Yankee donned an AL record nine GGs from 1985-94.
9. Continuing the tradition of great-fielding first sackers for the Dodgers, which essentially monopolized the award at first for two decades, this 1974 MVP fielded four GGs in the '70s.
10. If any player not in the Hall of Fame is more deserving of enshrinement, it's this player. He finished in the top 20 in MVP voting eight out of eleven years from 1949-59, hit 370 career homers and managed the 1969 Mets to a miraculous championship, along with winning three GGs. Name this great Dodger player.

GOLD GLOVE FIRST BASEMEN (ANSWERS)

1. Mark Grace

2. Keith Hernandez

3. George Scott

4. Vic Power

5. J.T. Snow

6. Bill White

7. Wes Parker

8. Don Mattingly

9. Steve Garvey

10. Gil Hodges

DOUBLE TIME

You're halfway home if you can answer these questions involving great doubles hitters.

1. Texas-born means no stranger to open spaces. This HOF center fielder holds a record with 793 career doubles, hit in AL parks from 1907-28. Like Barry Bonds in HRs, you're required to know this fact if you're going to walk into a sports bar.

2. Early twentieth-century Philly and Cleveland great had a complex about two-baggers, rapping out 648 to go along with a .340 career average.

3. Number two on the all-time list is this man, who, along with a bevy of singles, had 746 doubles, one-fifth of his career hits total.

4. This St. Louis slugger had an amazing 725 doubles, one more than Ty Cobb. These, along with 475 HRs, made for a strong slugging cocktail.

5. This Astro hit 668 doubles, topping out with a season-best 56 in 1999.

6. From 1973 to 1993, this AL HOFer connected on 665 pitches that carried him on a royal procession from home to second.

7. More than 700 HRs makes for plenty of base running. This man stopped to catch his breath halfway to home 624 times.

8. This man is locked in trivia lore for slinging 67 doubles in 1934. His next highest season total was a mere 30 in a short seven-year career with the Red Sox. Yet, like question one, this is an arrow you need in your trivia quiver.

9. This HOFer hit 605 doubles, a bigger number than his less caustic brother/teammate who only had fewer than half that amount. Pitchers had no antidote to the former's rampant two-bagging over twenty seasons from 1926-45.

10. With the option of a short green wall to rap balls off in left, and tricky spots to slip in stuff in right, he wound up at second 646 times between 1961 and 1983.

DOUBLE TIME (ANSWERS)

1. Tris Speaker

2. Nap Lajoie

3. Pete Rose

4. Stan Musial

5. Craig Biggio

6. George Brett

7. Hank Aaron

8. Earl Webb

9. Paul Waner

10. Carl Yastrzemski

Who's the Last...

1. Player to win the Triple Crown?

2. National Leaguer to hit .400?

3. National Leaguer to win 30 games in a season?

4. AL West team to win the World Series?

5. Pitcher to strike out 20 batters in a game?

6. Pitcher to win the MVP Award?

7. National Leaguer to reach the 3,000-hit plateau?

8. Player to reach the 500 home run plateau?

9. Player to reach the 600 home run plateau?

10. Of the original 1962 New York Mets to play for the franchise?

WHO'S THE LAST... (ANSWERS)

1. Carl Yastrzemski, 1967

2. Bill Terry, 1930

3. Dizzy Dean, 1934

4. Los Angeles Angels of Anaheim, 2002

5. Randy Johnson, May 8, 2001

6. Dennis Eckersley, 1992

7. Craig Biggio, June 28, 2007

8. Gary Sheffield, April 17, 2009

9. Jim Thome, August 15, 2011

10. Ed Kranepool, 1979

BASEBALL LINEAGES: YANKEES CATCHERS

New York Yankees			
YEARS	CATCHER	YEARS	CATCHER
1929-43	1.?	1970-79	4.?
		1980-82	Rick Cerone
1944-45	Mike Garbark	1983-86	5.?
1946-47	A. Robinson	1987-92	5 Catchers
1948	Gus Niarhos		
1949-59	2.?	1993-95	Mike Stanley
		1996-97	6.?
		1998-2009	7.?
1960-66	3.?		
1967-69	Jake Gibbs	2010	F. Cervelli
		2011	8.?

BASEBALL LINEAGES: YANKEES CATCHERS (ANSWERS)

1. Bill Dickey

2. Yogi Berra

3. Elston Howard

4. Thurman Munson

5. Butch Wynegar

6. Joe Girardi

7. Jorge Posada

8. Russell Martin

LONG AND LOYAL (2ND INNING)

Another batch of players deserve recognition for loyalty to their franchise and longevity in general. You are given the team they played with for these many years, position(s) and span of years played. Name these loyal lifers.

1. Baltimore Orioles P, 1965-1984

2. Boston Red Sox OF, 1939-1960

3. Pittsburgh Pirates OF, 1955-1972

4. Baltimore Orioles SS/3B, 1981-2001

5. Milwaukee Brewers SS/OF, 1974-1993

6. San Diego Padres OF, 1982-2001

7. Houston Astros C/2B/OF, 1988-2007

8. Cleveland Indians P, 1936-1956

9. New York Mets 1B-OF, 1962-1979

10. Los Angeles Dodgers SS, 1969-1986

LONG AND LOYAL (2ND INNING ANSWERS)

1. Jim Palmer

2. Ted Williams

3. Roberto Clemente

4. Cal Ripken

5. Robin Yount

6. Tony Gwynn

7. Craig Biggio

8. Bob Feller

9. Ed Kranepool

10. Bill Russell

Nicknames (2nd Inning)

1. The Bird

2. Stretch

3. Mr. Cub

4. The Christian Gentleman

5. The Chairman of the Board

6. Meal Ticket

7. Bucketfoot

8. Master Melvin

9. Poosh 'Em Up

10. The Heater From Van Meter

11. The Flying Dutchman

12. The Peerless Leader

Nicknames (2nd Inning answers)

1. Mark Fidrych

2. Willie McCovey

3. Ernie Banks

4. Christy Mathewson

5. Whitey Ford

6. Carl Hubbell

7. Al Simmons

8. Mel Ott

9. Enos Slaughter

10. Bob Feller

11. Honus Wagner

12. Frank Chance

PRESIDENTIAL NAMES

The men in the following questions share a common name. All you need to do is guess that name.

1. Right fielder on 2004 Red Sox has same last name as only president to resign from office.

2. Peanut-farming Georgian and man who won 1993 WS with walk-off HR.

3. All-time WS wins leader and butter-footed Michigan gridiron star.

4. Man who broke color barrier has same middle name as the last name of two presidents.

5. 191 RBI brought this man fame, as did a 1919 Nobel Peace Prize for this president.

6. Twins' 20-game winner in 1965 helped team make WS that year. He's known by a fishy first name and has a last name in common with a Civil War General who drank like he was a fish.

7. An impressive 373 wins made this righty a HOFer, meeting the high expectations of his first and middle names, which match those of the only president to serve two non-consecutive terms.

8. Catcher on 1984 Padres has same name as the nation's only Catholic President.

9. A seven-time All-Star lefty for White Sox in '50s and '60s, he won more than 200 games. This president won office as the only man from New Hampshire ever to do so.

10. A tooth-picking middle infielder with double initials for first names or Olympic pinch runner for Finley's A's share names with Revolutionary War General and first Commander-in-Chief.

PRESIDENTIAL NAMES (ANSWERS)

1. Trot/Richard Nixon

2. Joe/Jimmy Carter

3. Whitey/Gerald Ford

4. Jackie Roosevelt Robinson/Teddy and FDR

5. Hack/Woodrow Wilson

6. Mudcat/Ulysses Grant

7. Grover Cleveland Alexander

8. Terry/John Kennedy

9. Billy/Franklin Pierce

10. UL/Herb/George Washington

JIMMIE FOXX ★★★ Played 1954–1976

James Emory Foxx was known for his slugging, but he still hit over .300 for nearly every year of his 20-year career. He captured the American League batting title twice: in 1933 with the Philadelphia Athletics (.356) and in 1938 with the Boston Red Sox (.349). Seventeenth on the all-time list for home runs with 534, Foxx compiled 12 consecutive years in which he hit more than 30 home runs. Foxx was inducted into the Baseball Hall of Fame in 1951.

CAREER STATISTICS

Batting average	.325
At bats	8,134
Hits	2,646
Doubles	458
Home runs	534
Runs scored	1,751
Runs batted in	1,922
Bases on balls	1,452

Jimmie Foxx, a Maryland farm boy, was discovered by Home Run Baker, the former Philadelphia Athletics' third baseman. Baker referred him to Athletics owner-manager Connie Mack out of loyalty to his former team. There he joined an impressive lineup that included Mickey Cochrane and Al Simmons.

Foxx led the American League in home runs four times, not an easy feat to accomplish while playing in the same league with Babe Ruth. In 1932, Foxx smashed 58 home runs despite being hampered by a late season injury to his wrist. He was traded to Boston in 1936 where he hit more than 30 home runs in five of the seven years with the Red Sox. In 1938, Foxx led the league in RBIs (175), bases on balls (119), batting average (.349), on base percentage (.462), slugging percentage (.704) and total bases (398). He was literally a one-man-wrecking crew. Fenway had a new monster—and he was standing at the plate!

Foxx won the Triple Crown in 1933, batting .356, with 48 home runs and 163 RBIs. From 1928 to 1930, Foxx and the Philadelphia Athletics supplanted the New York Yankees as the best team in the American League. The Athletics played in three consecutive World Series championships, winning the Series in 1928 and 1929. In three Series Foxx batted

When his major league career ended Jimmie Foxx coached the Fort Wayne Daisies, one of the new All-American Girls Professional Baseball League teams that was formed when many young men were still in the armed forces.

.350, .333, and .348, knocked four home runs, one triple and three doubles and posted a career postseason slugging percentage of .609

THE SLUGGERS

BASEBALL LINEAGES: CHICAGO CUBS SECOND SACKERS

The Cubs began the 1900s as one of baseball's finest teams, winning two World Series in the first decade of the new century. 1903 – the year we start our lineage here – was not only the year the Chicago Orphans changed their nickname to the Cubs, but it also marked the first full season of the franchise's first Hall of Fame second baseman, of which there have been four total. That quartet you'll have to name yourself, along with several other Cubs second sackers we've selectively slipped from the following sequence...

CHICAGO CUBS SECOND BASEMEN				
YEARS	SECOND BASEMAN	YEARS	SECOND BASEMAN	
		1941-42	Lou Stringer	
		1943	Eddie Stanky	
		1944-47	Don Johnson	
1903-13	1. ?	1948-50	3 players	
		1951-53	4. ?	
		1954-56	Gene Baker	
1914-19	5 players	1957-60	3 players	
1920-22	Zeb Terry	1961	5. ?	
		1962-63	6. ?	
1923-28	4 players	1964	Joey Amalfitano	
1929-31	2. ?	1965-73	7. ?	
1932-40	3. ?			

CHICAGO CUBS SECOND BASEMEN	
YEARS	SECOND BASEMAN
1974	Vic Harris
1975-79	8.?
1979-82	3 players
1983-97	9.?
1998-2011	11 players

BASEBALL LINEAGES: CHICAGO CUBS SECOND SACKERS (ANSWERS)

1. Johnny Evers

2. Rogers Hornsby

3. Billy Herman

4. Eddie Miksis

5. Don Zimmer

6. Ken Hubbs

7. Glenn Beckert

8. Manny Trillo

9. Ryne Sandberg

CONSECUTIVE HITTING STREAKS

Name the following players who either precipitated a consistent batting
performance or had a hand in preventing their perpetuation.

1. Don Mattingly (1987) and Ken Griffey Jr. (1993) tied this man's record
   for consecutive games – eight – with a homer. This longball hitter
   performed the feat for the Pirates in 1956.

2. This sweet swinger holds the official modern-era records for reaching base
   in consecutive games (84) and at-bats (16).

3. In 1952, this towering former ROY tied Pinky Higgins' 1938 record for
   12 consecutive plate appearances with a hit after a midseason trade from
   the Red Sox to the Yankees. The 12 hits came in two amazing
   performances – a 5-5 game followed with a 7-7 effort the next day.

4. Willie Keeler holds the record for most consecutive seasons (eight) with
   200-plus hits. What slugger holds the record for most 150-plus hit
   seasons in a row (1955-71)?

5. Who holds the record for most seasons in a row (13) with 30 HRs?

6. In 1976, this HOFer tied the record for most games with three or more
   hits in a row with six. Games like these helped toward a regal .333 average,
   good enough to be crowned AL batting camp that year.

7. This eagle-eyed HOF hitter is best known for not striking out. In fact, he
   set a consecutive game record for not doing it in 115 contests while
   playing for Cleveland in the '20s. Being 5 foot 6 helped.

8. The record for a batter striking out in consecutive at-bats is 12. Not
   surprisingly, it was a pitcher getting a taste of his own medicine. The year
   was 1955, and although his team won the World Series, the rookie was a
   few years away from administering four consecutive years of the most
   powerful medicine baseball had ever seen.

9. A must mention – before hitting the big leagues, he hit in 61 straight
   games with the San Francisco Seals of the Pacific Coast League.

10. On July 17, 1941, pitchers Al Smith and Jim Bagby stymied Joe
    DiMaggio's 56-game hitting streak. Cleveland's third baseman made two
    terrific plays on lined shots to his left. DiMaggio himself said they were two
    of his hardest struck balls during the streak. Who was this record-snapping
    glove man?

Consecutive Hitting Streaks (answers)

1. Dale Long

2. Ted Williams

3. Walt Dropo

4. Hank Aaron

5. Barry Bonds

6. George Brett

7. Joe Sewell

8. Sandy Koufax

9. Joe DiMaggio

10. Ken Keltner

FRANCHISE'S LAST 20-GAME WINNER

Winning 20 games is the hallmark of a superb season for the modern pitcher. But what was once a common feat has become a statistical anomaly. The 1970s featured a combined ninety-six 20-game seasons by fifty-three different pitchers. In the past ten years, there have been a mere thirty-three 20-game seasons amongst only twenty-five different pitchers – and two years (2006 and 2009) in which no pitcher reached the mark. In fact, nearly half of MLB franchises have yet to field a 20-game winner this century.

By now you understand your obligation: name the last 20-game winner for each of the franchises listed below.

	TEAM	LAST YEAR
1.	Milwaukee Brewers	1986
2.	New York Mets	1990
3.	Pittsburgh Pirates	1991
4.	San Diego Padres	1978
5.	San Francisco Giants	1993
6.	Montreal Expos	1978
7.	Chicago Cubs	2001
8.	Cincinnati Reds	1988
9.	Florida Marlins	2005
10.	Houston Astros	2005

FRANCHISE'S LAST 20-GAME WINNER (1ST INNING ANSWERS)

1. Teddy Higuera

2. Frank Viola

3. John Smiley

4. Gaylord Perry

5. Bill Swift and John Burkett

6. Ross Grimsley

7. Jon Lieber

8. Danny Jackson

9. Dontrelle Willis

10. Roy Oswalt

ALMA MATERS

Each group of players below attended the same college, famously so. Name the college.

1. Reggie Jackson, Sal Bando, Barry Bonds, Dustin Pedroia

2. Coot Veal, Bo Jackson, Frank Thomas, Tim Hudson

3. Jackie Robinson, Todd Zeile, Troy Glaus

4. Jim Lonborg, Jack McDowell, Mike Mussina

5. Tom Seaver, Bill Lee, Mark McGwire

6. George Sisler, Charlie Gehringer, Barry Larkin, Jim Abbott

7. Greg Vaughn, Pat Burrell, Charles Johnson, Ryan Braun

8. Kevin Brown, Jason Varitek, Nomar Garciaparra

9. Cap Anson, Carl Yastrzemski, Craig Counsell

10. Bobby Thigpen, Rafael Palmeiro, Will Clark, Jonathan Papelbon

11. Lou Gehrig, Eddie Collins, Gene Larkin

12. Frank Viola, John Franco, Rich Aurilia

ALMA MATERS (ANSWERS)

1. Arizona State University

2. Auburn University

3. University of California, Los Angeles

4. Stanford University

5. University of Southern California

6. University of Michigan

7. University of Miami

8. Georgia Tech

9. University of Notre Dame

10. Mississippi State University

11. Columbia University

12. St. John's University

ROGERS HORNSBY ★★★ Played 1915–1937

CAREER STATISTICS

Rogers "Rajah" Hornsby batted higher than .300 for 19 years, including a batting average of more than .400 in four seasons. He won the Triple Crown twice and is second to Ty Cobb on the all-time average list with .358. From 1920 to 1925 Hornsby won six consecutive National League batting titles, averaging .397 and 42 doubles per season among his 1,296 hits in 3,268 at bats. Considered the greatest right-

Batting average	.358
At bats	8,173
Hits	2,930
Doubles	541
Triples	169
Home runs	301
Runs scored	1,579
Runs batted in	1,584
Bases on balls	1,038

handed hitter ever, Hornsby was inducted into the Baseball Hall of Fame in 1942.

Rogers Hornsby was born in Winters, Texas, on April 27, 1896. His mother named him Rogers because it was her maiden name. He broke into the major leagues in 1915 with the St. Louis Cardinals but did not hit his stride as a prolific hitter until 1919 when he began a streak of 13 consecutive seasons of batting .300 or higher.

Hornsby was always the first player to arrive at the ballpark. He had little interest outside of baseball. Hornsby once said, "People ask me what I do in the winter when there's no baseball. I'll tell you what I do. I stare out the window and wait for spring." As a hitter, his single mindedness paid off. He won the batting crown seven times in his career, with every one of those crowns earned with an average of .370 or higher.

Hornsby had seven 200-hit seasons, including 250 hits in 1922 when he led the league in total bases with 450. An incredible 40 percent of his hits (42 home runs, 14 triples, 46 doubles) went for extra bases. In 1924, he had a single season average of .424, the highest of the 20th century. Hornsby's career included several years as a player-manager. He played and managed for the St. Louis Cardinals, New York Giants, Boston Braves, Chicago Cubs and St. Louis Browns.

Rogers Hornsby had unorthodox ideas about which activities would diminish his hitting skills. He refused to attend the movies, read books or even a newspaper because he believed it would weaken his eyesight.

THE HITTERS

MADE LAST OUT OF WORLD SERIES

What worse feeling is there than being the last out of a baseball game? Answer: making the last out of an entire baseball season. The following players had the unfortunate distinction of ending a World Series at the plate. As you'll see, many involve well-known players and interesting circumstances.

1. This Sox second-sacker couldn't come through with another hit to add to the record 24 he rapped throughout fourteen postseason games in 1986. Jesse Orosco fanned him to bring a Game 7 end to the fated sequence of series events suffered by Boston.

2. With the tying run on deck and the bases loaded, Lew Burdette locked in his Series MVP performance by getting this Yankee to ground out to Eddie Matthews and give Milwaukee its only WS win, in 1957. This batter had not appeared in the Series since the third inning of Game 1 when back pain took his capable bat out of the lineup.

3. The Yankees elected to pitch to this future HOFer with two on in the ninth inning of a 1-0 Game 7. The batter ripped a Ralph Terry pitch right at shortstop Bobby Richardson to end the Series. This mammoth slugger would later admit it was the hardest ball he'd ever hit.

4. Cleon Jones caught the fly ball for the last out of the 1969 WS off the bat of this man who would skipper the Mets to a championship seventeen years later.

5. In 1955, a rookie Yankee at the start of an exceptional postseason career finally grounded out to Pee Wee Reese and preserved Johnny Podres' second shutout of the Series. The 6-to-1 out on the scorecard locked down Brooklyn's first championship since 1900, when it went by the name "Superbas."

6. The 1975 Red Sox frittered away an early 3-0 lead in Game 7. The Reds scored the eventual game-winning fourth run in the top of the ninth. This grand Red Sox soldier flied out to end the Series.

7. During the Yankees/Cardinals 1926 Series match-up, Game 7 came down to a one-run ball game in the ninth. Untrue to his form, this HOF Yankee decided to steal second in the bottom of the inning with two out. The catcher's throw to Rogers Hornsby resulted in the only World Series to end with a CS scorecard entry. To whom did Hornsby apply this famous tag?

8. Boston closer Keith Foulke fielded the ball off the bat of this Cardinal to end the 2004 WS and end an eighty-six-year championship drought that began as far back as when Babe Ruth wore a Red Sox uniform. The batter spookily bore Babe Ruth's number 3 on the back of his uniform, and would join the Red Sox the following year for one unfortunate, error-marred year.

9. In 1903, during the first championship series between the National and American leagues, this HOFer had a terrible performance to represent the Senior Circuit, making six errors and striking out to end Game 8 (series was best-of-nine) and give the Red Sox a come-from-behind series win.

10. They were the last of the original sixteen AL/NL franchises to win a World Series title, securing the 1980 championship. Tug McGraw, with the bases loaded, closed the door on the Royals by striking out this man, who, after a 230-hit season, set a World Series record by fanning 12 times in one series. Will you close out this category with a correct answer?

MADE LAST OUT OF WORLD SERIES (ANSWERS)

1. Marty Barrett

2. Moose Skowron

3. Willie McCovey

4. Davey Johnson

5. Elston Howard

6. Carl Yastrzemski

7. Babe Ruth

8. Edgar Renteria

9. Honus Wagner

10. Willie Wilson

LOU GEHRIG ★★★ Played 1923–1939

CAREER STATISTICS

Henry Louis "the Iron Horse" Gehrig was one-half of the Ruth-Gehrig one-two punch of the New York Yankees in the 1920s. In his 17-year career, Gehrig batted over .300 fourteen times and smacked more than 20 home runs in 13 seasons. He led the American League in every hitting category at least once and set a record for consecutive games played that lasted until 1995. He also set the record for career grand slams with 23. He was inducted into the Baseball Hall of Fame in 1939.

Batting average	.340
At bats	8,001
Hits	2,721
Doubles	535
Triples	162
Home runs	493
Runs scored	1,888
Runs batted in	1,990
Bases on balls	1,508

Lou Gehrig was born Ludwig Heinrich Gehrig in 1903 in New York City, the only child of his parents to survive childhood. His parents hoped that he would get his education from Columbia University where his father was fraternity caretaker. Gehrig enrolled in Columbia and excelled as a freshman playing baseball and football. The New York Yankees noticed and sign him to a professional contract.

In his illustrious major league career Gehrig hit more than 40 home runs five times and batted higher than .350 six times. He won the Triple Crown in 1934, batting .363, slamming 49 home runs, and driving in 165 RBIs. Except for his first year, he never had less than 100 runs or RBIs. Gehrig led the league in RBIs five times, runs four times, walks three times, home runs three times, double twice, slugging average twice, hits once, and batting average once.

In 1931 Lou Gehrig tied Babe Ruth for the home run title with 46. However, he'd actually hit 47 that year. One didn't count when he was tagged out for passing the base runner in front of him, who made the mistake of running off the field rather than crossing the plate.

On May 2, 1939 Gehrig took himself out of the lineup for the first time in 14 years. He went to the Mayo Clinic to find out why he wasn't feeling well and unable to perform on the diamond. Gehrig's diagnosis was devastating: amyotrophic lateral sclerosis. It was a rare disease with no cure. He retired on July 4, 1939 and died two years later on June 2, 1941.

THE SLUGGERS

TEAMMATES FOR THE AGES

For each question below, name the two players who appeared on the same roster together for at least fifteen years. Their long careers hint at their diamond prowess and the franchise for which they starred. You'll find many Hall of Famers in this lot.

1. This double play combo has played more games together than any pair of teammates in MLB history. From 1977-95, they were a fixture in Detroit and instrumental in bringing a World Series Championship to the city in 1984.

2. Cubs fans will always remember these two men in the same lineup. One is a Hall of Famer, the other a third basemen with a considerable amount of HOF supporters. Name these close-knit Cubbies who hold the NL record for teammates playing together.

3. What two Phillies Hall of Famers played on the team for fifteen straight years from 1972-86? One hit, the other pitched.

4. George Brett came up to the bigs in 1973 along with another infielder and a newly acquired hitter to fill the Royals' new DH slot. The three would play together for the next fifteen seasons and total twenty-one All-Star Games amongst them as fixtures on Kansas City's playoff entries in the 1970s and '80s. Who were these two Brett-brethren?

5. These two Brewers lifers formed Milwaukee's double play tandem for the first nine of their seventeen years together. The SS would be moved to CF and make the HOF after retiring. The second baseman was a local favorite from Fond du Lac, Wisconsin, who played at the University of Wisconsin-Oshkosh. Name these two Brew Crew players.

6. These two Reds greats played together in the 1970s, parted ways, reconvened on the 1983 Phillies to win another pennant, and then went back to the Reds for three seasons before retiring together. One made the HOF after a long wait and the other is still waiting for permission to enter.

7. Starting in 1956, two Pirates played together for sixteen years before their careers ended in 1972. They were key pieces to bringing a World Series Championship to Pittsburgh in 1960, and today each are in the Hall of Fame. Interestingly, they were voted in nearly thirty years apart – one in 1973 and the other in 2001.

8. Another two Pirates played together for fourteen years from 1927-40 and were brought back as Bros' 'n Braves and again as Brooklyn bro-kin. Let's broker a few more facts here: They're both in the Hall of Fame and have the same mother. Name them.

9. The old New York Giants had their own pair of Hall of Famers cemented on rosters from 1928-43. One broke into the bigs at seventeen and would hit 500 taters in twenty-two seasons. The other, a lefty pitcher, won 253 games and two MVPs. Each came up gigantic in the 1933 World Series. One led the team in hits and slugging while the pitcher dominated the opposing Senators with two complete game wins and a 0.00 ERA in a 4-1 Series trouncing of their AL acquaintances.

10. A final Hall of Fame duo: From 1925-33, this slugger teamed with a lefty legend to star for the Philadelphia A's. After a stint apart, they joined again in Boston and played as Red Sox from 1936-41. By chance, the pitcher in question nine (also a lefty) joined this A's/Sox great and were voted into Cooperstown the same year, HOF class of 1947. Sure enough, the 500 home run hitters in each question also were enshrined in the same class, 1951. In all, this quartet represents the finest hitter and pitcher from each league during their era.

TEAMMATES FOR THE AGES (ANSWERS)

1. Lou Whitaker and Alan Trammell

2. Billy Williams and Ron Santo

3. Mike Schmidt and Steve Carlton

4. Frank White and Hal McRae

5. Robin Yount and Jim Gantner

6. Tony Perez and Pete Rose

7. Roberto Clemente and Bill Mazeroski

8. Paul Waner and Lloyd Waner

9. Carl Hubbell and Mel Ott

10. Lefty Grove and Jimmie Foxx

FAMOUS TRADES (2ND INNING)

Name the unnamed players traded on the following dates.

1. December 10, 1971: Young pitcher is traded by the New York Mets with Frank Estrada, Don Rose and Leroy Stanton to the California Angels for Jim Fregosi.

2. December 9, 1965: This great is sent by the Cincinnati Reds to the Baltimore Orioles for Milt Pappas, Jack Baldschun and Dick Simpson.

3. May 11, 1972: Aged legend is traded by the San Francisco Giants to the New York Mets for Charlie Williams and $50,000.

4. February 10, 2000: This '90s great is offered by the Seattle Mariners to the Cincinnati Reds for Mike Cameron, Brett Tomko, Antonio Perez and Jake Meyer.

5. December 4, 1988: Future HOFer is traded by the Baltimore Orioles to the Los Angeles Dodgers for Juan Bell, Brian Holton and Ken Howell.

6. July 29, 1989: Chicago White Sox send him with Fred Manrique to Texas Rangers for Scott Fletcher, Sammy Sosa and Wilson Alvarez.

7. December 10, 1981: He's traded by the San Diego Padres with a player to be named later and Steve Mura to the St. Louis Cardinals for Sixto Lezcano, Garry Templeton and a player to be named later.

8. January 3, 1920: This ballplayer is purchased by the New York Yankees from the Boston Red Sox for $100,000.

9. June 13, 1930: In the first-ever swap of former batting champions, the Senators give up this HOFer in exchange for the great Heinie Manush and budding pitching star General Crowder.

FAMOUS TRADES (2ND INNING ANSWERS)

1. Nolan Ryan

2. Frank Robinson

3. Willie Mays

4. Ken Griffey Jr.

5. Eddie Murray

6. Harold Baines

7. Ozzie Smith

8. Babe Ruth

9. Goose Goslin

TONY GWYNN ★★★ Played 1982–2001

Anthony Keith Gwynn played twenty years for the San Diego Padres, hitting higher than .300 in nineteen and compiling a career batting average of .338. Gwynn, who ranks fourteenth on the all-time batting average list, led the National League in batting eight times and had five 200-hit seasons. Gwynn was inducted into the Baseball Hall of Fame in 2007.

CAREER STATISTICS

Batting average	.338
At bats	9,288
Hits	3,141
Doubles	543
Runs scored	1,383
Runs batted in	1,138
Bases on balls	790

Like legendary Ted Williams, Tony Gwynn played a lot of baseball in San Diego. He attended San Diego State University, and then spent his entire career with the Padres. Gwynn batted .394 in 1994, the highest season average since Ted Williams batted .406 in 1941.

Unlike Williams, Gwynn in the 1980s and 1990s got to play and distinguish himself in two World Series, two division championships and two league championship series, batting a combined .306 with 33 hits in 108 at-bats. He batted .500 in the Padres' four-game loss of the 1998 World Series to the New York Yankees, collecting eight hits including a home run.

Gwynn was a master practitioner of hitting. He developed offseason practice routines that honed his swing. In January of the offseason, Gwynn would hit fifty balls a day off a batting tee. In February, he took regular batting practice but practiced hitting the pitches where the hit would advance imaginary runners to third base and home. He focused on hitting pitches to the opposite field to ingrain "staying on the ball longer"–little things that paid big dividends for this baseball blue blood.

Despite his size (5 foot 11 and 215 pounds), Tony Gwynn used a relatively small bat—a 32½-inch, 31-ounce Louisville Slugger Model C-263, medium barrel and medium handle. He nicknamed this custom bat "The Peashooter."

THE HITTERS

BASEBALL LINEAGES: CARDINALS FIRST BASEMEN

Another great Senior Circuit franchise with a certified bunch of celebrity position players – St. Louis Cardinals first sackers. Many canonized by Cooperstown paced this sanctified domain of Cardinals, and several others here rank as the best hitters and fielders of their era. The deck is stacked, but play your Cards right and you'll win big in this category.

ST. LOUIS CARDINALS FIRST BASEMEN			
YEARS	FIRST BASEMAN	YEARS	FIRST BASEMAN
1882-91	1. ?	1923-31	3. ?
1894-96	Roger Connor	1932-35	Ripper Collins
1897-1903	6 players	1936-41	4. ?
1904-07	2. ?		
		1942-45	Ray Sanders
1908-13	Ed Konetchy	1946-47	5. ?
1914-22	4 players	1948-54	5 players
		1955-59	

ST. LOUIS CARDINALS FIRST BASEMEN			
YEARS	**FIRST BASEMAN**	**YEARS**	**FIRST BASEMAN**
		1988	Bob Horner
1960-65	**6.?**	1989-92	Pedro Guerrero
		1993-94	Gregg Jefferies
		1995-96	John Mabry
1966-68	**7.?**	1997-2001	**10.?**
1969	Joe Torre		
1970-72	2 players	2002-03	Tino Martinez
1973-74	Torre	2004-11	**11.?**
1975	Ron Fairly		
1976-83	**8.?**		
1984	David Green		
1985-87	**9.?**		

BASEBALL LINEAGES: CARDINALS FIRST BASEMEN (ANSWERS)

1. Charlie Comiskey

2. Jake Beckley

3. Jim Bottomley

4. Johnny Mize

5. Stan Musial

6. Bill White

7. Orlando Cepeda

8. Keith Hernandez

9. Jack Clark

10. Mark McGwire

11. Albert Pujols

FILL IN THE LINEUP (2ND INNING)

Who's missing from the batting lineup of these famous orders? Lineups are listed as the most frequent orders submitted by the manager for that season.

1959 Chicago White Sox
Game 1, '59 World Series

1. ? SS
2. ? 2B
3. ? CF
4. T Kluszewski 1B
5. ? C
6. B Goodman 3B
7. A Smith LF
8. B Phillips RF
9. E Wynn P

1973 Oakland A's

1. ? SS
2. B North CF
3. ? 3B
4. R Jackson RF
5. D Johnson DH
6. ? LF
7. ? 1B
8. R Fosse C
9. D Green 2B

1975 Boston Red Sox

Name the missing players from this, the starting lineup for Game 6 of the '75 World Series

1. C Cooper 1B
2. ? 2B
3. C Yastrzemski LF
4. C Fisk C
5. ? CF
6. ? 3B
7. D Evans RF
8. ? SS
9. L Tiant P

FILL IN THE LINEUP (2ND INNING ANSWERS)

1959 White Sox	**1973 Oakland A's**
1. Luis Aparicio SS	1. Bert Campaneris SS
2. Nellie Fox 2B	2. B North CF
3. Jim Landis CF	3. Sal Bando 3B
4. T Kluszewski 1B	4. R Jackson RF
5. Sherm Lollar C	5. D Johnson DH
6. B Goodman 3B	6. Joe Rudi LF
7. Al Smith LF	7. Gene Tenace 1B
8. B Phillips RF	8. R Fosse C
9. E Wynn P	9. D Green 2B

1975 Boston Red Sox
1. C Cooper 1B
2. Denny Doyle 2B
3. C Yastrzemski LF
4. C Fisk C
5. Fred Lynn CF
6. Rico Petrocelli 3B
7. D Evans RF
8. Rick Burleson SS
9. L Tiant P

TEAMS THEY PITCHED FOR (2ND INNING)

Rack 'em up again: The following pitchers were much traveled, playing for different teams with various degrees of success. Each had remarkable stints with at least three squads, if not more. Name at least three of those teams for which they pitched. An extra point for each team you can name past three.

1. Goose Gossage

2. Lee Smith

3. Orel Hershiser

4. Bert Blyleven

5. Jamie Moyer

6. Luis Tiant

7. Tom Seaver

8. Dwight Gooden

9. Frank Viola

10. Mike Morgan

Teams They Pitched For (2nd Inning answers)

1. White Sox, Pirates, Yankees, Padres, Cubs, Giants, Rangers, A's, Mariners

2. Cubs, Red Sox, Cardinals, Yankees, Orioles, Angels, Reds, Expos

3. Dodgers, Indians, Giants, Mets

4. Twins, Rangers, Pirates, Indians, Angels

5. Cubs, Rangers, Cardinals, Orioles, Red Sox, Mariners, Phillies

6. Indians, Twins, Red Sox, Yankees, Pirates, Angels

7. Mets, Reds, White Sox, Red Sox

8. Mets, Yankees, Indians, Astros, Devil Rays

9. Twins, Mets, Red Sox, Reds, Blue Jays

10. A's, Yankees, Blue Jays, Mariners, Orioles, Dodgers, Cubs, Cardinals, Reds, Twins, Rangers

POSTSEASON VETERANS (1ST INNING)

The following players had significant roles on multiple playoff teams. Their years in playoffs and teams they appeared with are given as clues. Name these postseason veterans.

1.

1B/DH
1991-93 Blue Jays
1999 Mets
2000-01 Mariners
2004 Yankees
2005 Red Sox

2.

OF/IF
1983, 2000 White Sox
1990, 1992 A's
1997 Orioles
1999 Indians

3.

C
1987 Cardinals
1990 Red Sox
1995 Indians

4.

P
1984, 1987 Tigers
1991 Twins
1992 Blue Jays

5.

SS/2B
1985, 1989, 1993 Blue Jays
1995 Yankees
1997 Indians

6.

2B
1972-73, 75-76, 79 Reds
1980 Astros
1983 Phillies

POSTSEASON VETERANS (1ST INNING ANSWERS)

1. John Olerud

2. Harold Baines

3. Tony Pena

4. Jack Morris

5. Tony Fernandez

6. Joe Morgan

NAME'S THE SAME (2ND INNING)

The following men all have a name in common. Name that name.

1. Doug, Randy, Sam

2. Jack, Tony, Will

3. Buck, Steve, Kenny

4. Sam, Del, Jim

5. Russ, Ramon, David

6. Josh, Bob, Kirk

7. Gary, Joe, Lance

8. Mike, Damaso, Freddy

9. Mort, Scott, Cecil

10. Fleet, Gee, Dixie, Larry

11. Joe, Wilbur, Kerry

12. Elston, Frank, Ryan

NAME'S THE SAME (2ND INNING ANSWERS)

1. Jones

2. Clark

3. Rogers

4. Rice

5. Ortiz

6. Gibson

7. Carter

8. Garcia

9. Cooper

10. Walker

11. Wood

12. Howard

Multiple Rings, Multiple Teams

The following players have won at least one World Series with two different franchises. Based on the information provided, name the players who've had the privilege of contributing to more than one winning team. Note: In rare cases, the player may not have played in the World Series one year, but made significant regular season contributions to their team.

1. This HOF third baseman was an integral part of the 1957 Milwaukee title team, but is not popularly known for winning another title as a late-season veteran addition to the Tigers in 1968, his last year in the majors.

2. Another HOFer, this star pitcher won an amazing five World Series in the 1970s, all with AL teams. Who was this hunter & gatherer of title rings?

3. Sweet dreams are made of this guy's even rarer distinction of winning rings with three different teams. Here are the teams, chronologically: the Los Angeles Dodgers, Oakland A's and Toronto Blue Jays. Name this pitcher.

4. AYU is not giving you a time frame here. This All-Star right fielder won four rings with the Yankees after winning a title with the Reds. Considering the periods of time in which this feat could happen, narrow down your decades and find the answer.

5. Remember this spunky Notre Dame-bred infielder from the 1997 Marlins and 2001 Diamondbacks? He scored the winning run in the eleventh inning of the '97 Series and came up huge as 2001 NLCS MVP for the Diamondbacks. Counsel with your uncle if you're stuck on the answer.

6. Three pitchers from the 1992 Blue Jays Championship team played vital roles in the starting pitching rotations of the Yankees title teams later in the decade. Can you name all three?

7. This huge lefty slugger was an All-Star in three decades and won rings with the Pirates and A's ten years apart. Can you name him?

8. This Pontiac-born bruiser starred for the World Series Champion Tigers in 1984. Then, despite an injury that limited him to one at-bat in the 1988 Series he hit what might be the greatest home run of all time.

9. Two all-time greats spurred the Red Sox to victory in 1912 and 1915, then showed up on the Cleveland roster for its 1920 championship. One may be the greatest center fielder of all time and the other was a pitcher who, after throwing out his arm with the Sox, redefined his career as an outfielder, posting a .297 average with 432 hits and 275 RBI for Cleveland from 1917 to 1922. Name these greats.

Multiple RINGS, Multiple TEAMS

1. Eddie Matthews

2. Catfish Hunter

3. Dave Stewart

4. Paul O'Neill

5. Craig Counsell

6. David Cone, Jimmy Key and David Wells

7. Dave Parker

8. Kirk Gibson

9. Tris Speaker and Smoky Joe Wood

JOE DIMAGGIO ★★★ Played 1936–1951

Joseph Paul "Joltin' Joe" DiMaggio holds the record for hitting safely in 56 consecutive games. In all but two of his 13 seasons he batted over .300, retiring with a lifetime average of .325. He compiled double-digit home run totals every year of his career, and he led the American League twice each in average, home runs, and RBIs. He was inducted into the Baseball Hall of Fame in 1955.

CAREER STATISTICS

Batting average	.325
At bats	6,821
Hits	2,214
Doubles	389
Home runs	361
Runs scored	1,390
Runs batted in	1,537
Bases on balls	790

Joltin' Joe DiMaggio, also called the Yankee Clipper, played center field for the New York Yankees for 13 years. In ten of those years he helped bring the Bronx Bombers to the World Series where the Yankees emerged as world champions nine times. Those DiMaggio-led Yankee teams were so dominant in Series play that only one time in 10 appearances did the Yankees need seven games to win. In the three Series in which the Yankees swept (won 4 games to none)—in 1938 vs. the Cubs, in 1939 vs. the Reds, and in 1950 vs. the Phillies—DiMaggio batted a combined average of .304 and smashed three home runs. He was a player of great consistency and consistently great when playing on baseball's biggest stage.

DiMaggio was the middle of three baseball-playing brothers—Dom, Joe and Vince—and the eighth of nine children. Their parents, Italian immigrants who settled in San Francisco, weren't too enthusiastic about their boys' obsession with baseball. However, their love of the game and talent eventually paid off—especially for Joe. As a teenaged player, he performed tremendously for the San Francisco Seals, batting .340 with 28 home runs and 169 RBIs at age 18.

When he joined the Yankees in 1936 at age 22 he hit .323, with 29 home runs and 125 RBIs, and he led the league in triples with 15. In 1939 DiMaggio won the first of his three MVP awards. In 1941, DiMaggio achieved his greatest feat. From May 15, when

Joe DiMaggio was a shy, private person. According to Hank Greenberg, "If he said hello to you, that was a long conversation."

he went 1-for-4 against the Chicago White Sox, until July 17, he hit in 56 consecutive games.

THE HITTERS

BASEBALL LINEAGES: CLEVELAND CENTER FIELDERS

Another prolific position for a particular team. Your first four answers should be Hall of Famers. Some nods to the old Municipal Stadium fans as well.

CLEVELAND CENTER FIELDERS			
YEARS	CF	YEARS	CF
1901	Ollie Pickering	1939-47	5 players
1902-05	Harry Bay		
1906	Elmer Flick	1948-55	3. ?
1907-12	Joe Birmingham		
1913-15	Nemo Leibold		
1916-26	1. ?	1956	Steve Busby
		1957	4. ?
		1958	
		1959-62	Jimmy Piersall
1927-28	2 players	1963-68	5. ?
1929-38	2. ?	1969-72	4 players
		1973-75	George Hendrick

CLEVELAND CENTER FIELDERS	
YEARS	CF
1976-82	6.?
1983	Gorman Thomas
1984-87	7.?
1988-89	Joe Carter
1990	Mitch Webster
1991	Alex Cole
1992-96	8.?
1997	Marquis Grissom
1998-2001	
2002-03	Milton Bradley
2004-11	9.?

BASEBALL LINEAGES: CLEVELAND CENTER FIELDERS (ANSWERS)

1. Tris Speaker

2. Earl Averill

3. Larry Doby

4. Roger Maris

5. Vic Davalillo

6. Rick Manning

7. Brett Butler

8. Kenny Lofton

9. Grady Sizemore

REAL FIRST NAMES (2ND INNING)

What are the actual first names of the following players with these famous monikers?

1. Catfish Hunter

2. Yogi Berra

3. Babe Ruth

4. Cap Anson

5. Chipper Jones

6. Coco Crisp

7. Three Finger Brown

8. Satchel Paige

9. Goose Gossage

10. Lou Gehrig

REAL FIRST NAMES (2ND INNING ANSWERS)

1. James (Jim)

2. Lawrence

3. George

4. Adrian (middle name Constantine)

5. Larry

6. Covelli

7. Mordecai

8. Leroy

9. Rich(ard)

10. Henry

ROBERTO CLEMENTE ★★★ Played 1955-1972

Roberto Walker Clemente is a member of the 3,000 hits club, with exactly 3,000. His lifetime batting average is .317. Clemente won the National League batting title four times, and in 13 of his 18 seasons with the Pittsburgh Pirates, he batted over .300. Clemente was inducted into the Baseball Hall of Fame in a special election in 1973.

CAREER STATISTICS

Batting average	.317
At bats	9,454
Hits	3,000
Doubles	440
Home runs	240
Runs scored	1,416
Runs batted in	1,305
Bases on balls	621

Roberto Clemente played with the Pittsburgh Pirates his entire career, hitting over .300 for 13 of his 18 seasons. He collected 200 or more hits in four seasons, won four batting titles, and a MVP award in 1966. Clemente led the Pirates to two spectacular seven-game World Series championships, in 1960 and 1971. Clemente batted .310 and .414 respectively. In the 1971 Series against the Baltimore Orioles, Clemente banged out 12 hits, getting at least one hit in each game, and slugged two home runs.

Clemente was a slashing line-drive hitter rather than a power hitter. The fences at Forbes Field were deep and worked against all but the most powerful players who played there (the lone exception was slugger Ralph Kiner, who led the league in home runs in the seven years he played in Forbes Field). Clemente, who stood a good distance away from the plate, simply reached out and smashed the ball to right-center field when pitchers tried to throw strikes on the outside corner.

Clemente was not only a great baseball player but also a noble humanitarian and role model for youngsters. He started the construction of "Sports City" in Puerto Rico, where youngsters could learn to play. He assisted Puerto Rico's efforts to aid Nicaraguans who had suffered a devastating earthquake. When he died in a tragic plane crash on December 31, 1972, he was taking emergency supplies to Nicaragua.

The Brooklyn Dodgers originally signed Roberto Clemente to his first professional baseball contract in 1952. He came over to the Pirates from the Dodgers in the 1954 Rule 5 draft when Pirates general manager Branch Rickey picked him, thus giving Rickey credit for having drafted the major league baseball's first Hispanic star.

THE HITTERS

FIRST TO MAKE THESE AMOUNTS OF MONEY

Free agency in the 1970s saw the dam bust on baseball salaries, making the average baseball contract the most lucrative in all of sports. The following players reached salary milestones for one season's worth of pay.

1. $50,000 (1922): "I know, but I had a better year than Hoover," was this player's retort to press comment about his salary exceeding that of then-President Herbert Hoover

2. $100,000 (1947): This Detroit slugger hit six figures after World War II

3. $500,000 (1977): A couple of years later and this Phillies Hall of Famer could have reaped benefits of an exploding free agent market

4. $1,000,000 (1979): Astros were first to spend seven figures to pry this pitcher away from Angels

5. $2,000,000 (1982): Slugger past his prime signed by Mets was dead weight for four and a half seasons before New York released him in August 1986 and won World Series two months later

6. $5,000,000 (1991): Texas Con Man sat fat on his money for five years before leaving in a huff for the Canadian border and never looked back – especially while being stuck in the arse with hypodermic needles by clubhouse staff

7. $10,000,000 (1996): Before the White Sox inked him for over $10 million per year, he was an angry young Cleveland OF who yelled at fifteen-year old me for calling him "Joey" before a game at Fenway Park. He was jogging back to the visitor's dugout, but stopped short to point at my face and tell me his new name through grit teeth. I nodded and looked down at the baseball card I was hoping he'd sign. It said JOEY, not the least cool new first name a person could choose. Plus it said Rookie Prospect on it – not Hypersensitive, Terrible Name-Choosing Sociopath. Things only got worse when I mistook Jesse Orosco for Tom Candiotti. He ignored me but

was visibly tearing as he descended into the dugout. Minutes later Brook Jacoby came out and chastised the entire group of fans lingering near the dugout, screaming "Everyone with bad skin throws a knuckleball?"

8. $15,000,000 (1998): Free-agent pitcher inked away from Padres by Dodgers

9. $20,000,000 (2000): Red Sox seemed to hit apex of salary signing

10. $25,000,000 (2000): Red Sox $20-million signing is trumped hours later when Rangers lavish this prima donna with a ten-year, quarter-billion contract

FIRST TO MAKE THESE AMOUNTS OF MONEY (ANSWERS)

1. Babe Ruth

2. Hank Greenberg

3. Mike Schmidt

4. Nolan Ryan

5. George Foster

6. Roger Clemens

7. Albert Belle

8. Kevin Brown

9. Manny Ramirez

10. Alex Rodriguez

FRANCHISE'S LAST 20-GAME WINNER (2ND INNING)

By now you understand your obligation: name the last 20-game winner for each of the franchises listed below. The year should clue you in, or at least trigger memories of landscape-format baseball cards with split-images of statistical leaders from each league.

	TEAM	LAST 20-GAME WINNER
1.	Detroit Tigers	2011
2.	Boston Red Sox	2007
3.	Los Angeles Angels	2005
4.	Baltimore Orioles	1984
5.	Kansas City Royals	1989
6.	Oakland A's	2002
7.	Seattle Mariners	2003
8.	Texas Rangers	1998
9.	Atlanta Braves	2003
10.	Chicago White Sox	2003

FRANCHISE'S LAST 20-GAME WINNER (2ND INNING ANSWERS)

1. Justin Verlander

2. Josh Beckett

3. Bartolo Colon

4. Mike Boddicker

5. Bret Saberhagen

6. Barry Zito

7. Jamie Moyer

8. Rick Helling

9. Russ Ortiz

10. Esteban Loaiza

CONSECUTIVE PITCHING STREAKS

Each question in this category singles out a record-setting pitcher who is laudable
for sustaining spectacular periods of success on the mound.

1. This New York Giant with 24 victories overlapping two seasons, 1936 and
   '37, set the record for successive wins.

2. Smilin' Timmy Keefe won 19 games in a row in 1888. Another HOFer
   tied this record for the Giants in 1912. Name him.

3. Though his consecutive scoreless inning streak was broken, this Dodger
   still holds the record for throwing the most consecutive shutouts with six,
   done over twenty days in 1968.

4. The aforementioned Dodger's total of 58 frames without allowing a run
   isn't a major league record. It's not even a Dodger franchise record.
   During his 1988 Cy Young year, he raised the bar on the scoreless steak,
   from 58 to 59 innings.

5. This all-time legend threw 24.1 consecutive hitless innings over three
   games. In the middle was a perfect game. It happened in 1904.

6. This mound artist set the record for most games in a row with 10 or more
   strikeouts – eight. The year was 1999, so don't say Nolan Ryan.

7. This be-goggled closer saved a record 84 straight games from 2002-04.

8. The last man also tied a record by K'ing 10 batters in row, but in multiple
   games as a closer. A starting pitcher set the record on one Amazin' day in
   1970.

9. A record seventeen seasons (1988-2004) of 15-plus wins – who did that?

10. This intrepid hurler started Opening Day a record fourteen years in a row
    from 1980-93, winning championship rings with three teams.

CONSECUTIVE PITCHING STREAKS (ANSWERS)

1. Carl Hubbell

2. Rube Marquard

3. Don Drysdale

4. Orel Hershiser

5. Cy Young

6. Pedro Martinez

7. Eric Gagne

8. Tom Seaver

9. Greg Maddux

10. Jack Morris

WADE BOGGS ★★★ Played 1982–1999

CAREER STATISTICS

Batting average	.328
At bats	9,180
Hits	3,010
Doubles	578
Home runs	118
Runs scored	1,513
Runs batted in	1,014
Bases on balls	1,412

Wade Anthony Boggs was a consistent line drive hitter, especially to the opposite field. He began his 18-year career in 1982 with the Boston Red Sox by averaging .356 for his first seven seasons. Boggs compiled more than 200 hits per season from 1983 through 1989 and led the American League in batting five times, including four consecutive seasons, 1985 to 1988, with successive averages of .368, .357, .363 and .366. He was inducted into the Baseball Hall of Fame in 2005.

The Boston Red Sox took notice of Wade Boggs when he played shortstop for his high school team in Tampa, Florida, earning the team's MVP. Boggs also earned All-Conference, All-State and All-America honors. He soon signed with the Red Sox after being drafted in the seventh round in 1976. After a six-year minor league career—in which he batted over .300 for five consecutive years—he was called up mid-season in 1982 to replace an injured player. In 104 games he batted .349, setting the American League rookie record. Playing in 153 games during the next season Boggs compiled the first of his seven consecutive 200-hit seasons and won the league batting title with a .361 average.

Wade Boggs was literally an on-base machine (he is ranked 21st all-time). He compiled four seasons in which he stroked more than 200 hits and earned more than 100 bases on balls.This surpassed the power hitting Babe Ruth, who accomplished this for three seasons, and was second only to Lou Gehrig, another power hitter who did it for seven seasons. In nine of Boggs' first ten seasons he averaged an on-base percentage of more then .400, including four seasons in which he reached base at a rate of .450 or better.

Wade Boggs was superstitious. His daily diet during the season was chicken. He believed that putting strawberries on his cheesecake led to bad luck. He ate his cheesecake without topping it with strawberries.

Boggs was traded to the New York Yankees in 1993, averaging .313 in five seasons and earning a world championship ring in 1996.

THE HITTERS

FRANCHISE LINEAGES: NEW YORK METS MANAGERS

In their short but dynamic history, the Mets dugout has been manned by several notable managers – for better or worse. Identify the missing skippers in this Metropolitan manifest.

NEW YORK METS MANAGERS			
YEARS	MANAGER	YEARS	MANAGER
		1976	Joe Frazier
1962-65	1.?	1977-81	4.?
1965-67	Wes Westrum	1982-83	George Bamberger
1967	Salty Parker	1983	Frank Howard
1968-71	2.?	1984-90	5.?
1972-75	3.?		
1975	Roy McMillan		

NEW YORK METS MANAGERS			
YEARS	**MANAGER**	**YEARS**	**MANAGER**
1990-91	Bud Harrelson	2003-04	Art Howe
1991	Mike Cubbage	2005-08	**7. ?**
1992-93	Jeff Torborg		
1993-96	Dallas Green	2008-10	Jerry Manuel
		2011	Terry Collins
1996-2002	**6. ?**		

FRANCHISE LINEAGES: NEW YORK METS MANAGERS (ANSWERS)

1. Casey Stengel

2. Gil Hodges

3. Yogi Berra

4. Joe Torre

5. Davey Johnson

6. Bobby Valentine

7. Willie Randolph

GREAT OPENING DAYS

We dedicate this page to the authors of stellar Opening Day performances.

1. 1986 boded well for the Red Sox when this player became the first ever to hit the first pitch of the season opener for a HR.

2. Who's the only pitcher to throw a no-hitter on Opening Day?

3. This player began the year with 3 HRs in 1988, following right where he left off after winning the 1987 AL MVP.

4. The only other time this feat happened was on April 4, 2005, when this man treated his Detroit fans to three round trippers. Who is this girthy player, popularly known as "Meat Hook?"

5. Another triple-homer Opening Day by this man gave Cubs fans hope that maybe 1994 was their year. Strangely, he ended his MLB career with only 13 dongs before fleeing to Japan and becoming one of that nation's greatest-ever HR hitters.

6. He never hit three, but this man did hit a total of 8 career HRs during season openers, along with 578 more on other dates. The 1975 season also started with this man in the Cleveland dugout as MLB's first-ever black manager.

7. This control pitcher keyed his team to seven Opening Day wins, a record for starting openers without a defeat.

8. Each of his nine Opening Day wins were shutouts. In 1910, he went 15 innings to blank the eventual World Champion A's.

9. In 1993, this pitcher took the mound at age forty-six to become oldest Opening Day starter in MLB history.

10. This team holds the record for best Opening Day win percentage at home – more than 75 percent. History has yet to get a firm grip on the scales of fortune of this relatively young franchise and balance out its lopsided rate of Opening Day wins.

Great Opening Days (answers)

1. Dwight Evans

2. Bob Feller

3. George Bell

4. Dmitri Young

5. Karl "Tuffy" Rhodes

6. Frank Robinson

7. Jimmy Key

8. Walter Johnson

9. Nolan Ryan

10. Toronto Blue Jays

INANIMATE OBJECTS

Do me a solid and grab hold of these answers. Each question here asks you to identify a ballplayer whose name is also an inanimate object. Inane category you say? Why thank you.

1. Hang your stockings on lucky number seven.
2. Packaged by the Pirates in an exchange for Phillie Jim Bunning, this young shortstop was moved to third base to make room for valued prospect Larry Bowa. Soon after, a young Mike Schmidt again made him expendable. Sent to Milwaukee as part of a seven-player deal, he invested himself as a Brewers regular for the next eleven seasons, four as an All-Star.
3. How to put this question lightly: A starter-turned-reliever, he went 11-0 from the pen for Toronto in 1985. He twice lost near no-hit bids, one courtesy of a Robin Yount ninth-inning single. Saw as many dark days as he did bright, with as many career wins as losses – 96.
4. Preferring the pitch to the pine, he copped a squat behind home and stayed put for seventeen prolific seasons in which he won two MVPs, two rings and ten Gold Gloves.
5. This moundsman Medusa'ed AL hitters in 1980 with a 25-7 Cy Young season. That one season pact with the devil left his arm a dead weight and put the grave marker on his pitching career.
6. A Pirate, Phillie, Expo and Padre, this second baseman had money seasons in '75 and '77, both times cracking 40 or more doubles.
7. This second baseman and 1982 NL Rookie of the Year was pivotal in bringing home a World Series trophy for the Dodgers in '88. Holds the Yankees record for singles in a season (171 in 1989).
8. Though this first overall pick in the 1976 amateur draft never broke a four-minute mile, he slid down 209 batters to lead the AL in Ks for the Mariners in 1982, his only All-Star appearance in fifteen seasons.
9. After floundering with the Mets, the Padres rang for this reliever, who soon pealed off three straight 40-save seasons from 2009-11.
10. This OF/DH has played for a record thirteen different MLB teams. His longest and most productive stint was his five years in Oakland. Oh, and he's Canadian; he's one of only two humans from that nation to hit more than 200 HRs. Did we mention the part about playing for a ton of teams? We did? Okay. Thirteen to be exact.

INANIMATE OBJECTS (ANSWERS)

1. Mickey Mantle

2. Don Money

3. Dennis Lamp

4. Johnny Bench

5. Steve Stone

6. Dave Cash

7. Steve Sax

8. Floyd Bannister

9. Heath Bell

10. Matt Stairs

FRANCHISE LINEAGES: OAKLAND A'S CLOSERS

Can you place the stoppers in the gaps in the following chronologies of commanding closers? Though relatively new on the landscape of Major League municipalities, each team has overcome instability by producing an heir to their distinguished line of relief royalty.

OAKLAND A'S			
YEARS	CLOSER	YEARS	CLOSER
1968	Jim Aker		
		1996-99	3. ?
1969-76	1. ?	2000-01	J. Isringhausen
		2002-04	3 RPs
		2005-08	4. ?
1977-84	7 RPs	2009-11	5. ?
1985-87	Jay Howell		
1988-95	2. ?		

FRANCHISE LINEAGES: OAKLAND A'S CLOSERS (ANSWERS)

1. Rollie Fingers

2. Dennis Eckersley

3. Billy Taylor

4. Huston Street

5. Andrew Bailey

HALL OF FAMER HOME STATES (2ND INNING)

Identify which state where each group of players below was born.

1. Reggie Jackson, Tommy Lasorda, Stan Musial, Roy Campanella

2. Nolan Ryan, Frank Robinson, Joe Morgan

3. Jim Bunning, Pee Wee Reese, Happy Chandler

4. Dave Winfield, Paul Molitor, Chief Bender

5. Grover Cleveland, Wade Boggs, Bob Gibson

6. Casey Stengel, Earl Weaver, Yogi Berra

7. Goose Goslin, Joe Medwick, Billy Hamilton

8. Luke Appling, Catfish Hunter, Gaylord Perry, Enos Slaughter

9. Johnny Bench, Mickey Mantle, Willie Stargell

10. Lou Brock, Dizzy Dean, Brooks Robinson

HALL OF FAMER HOME STATES (2ND INNING ANSWERS)

1. Pennsylvania

2. Texas

3. Kentucky

4. Minnesota

5. Nebraska

6. Missouri

7. New Jersey

8. North Carolina

9. Oklahoma

10. Arkansas

Postseason Veterans (2nd Inning)

Call them good luck charms, or just plain lucky, but the following well-traveled players landed on several playoff teams throughout their career. We give you each player's primary position(s) with the seasons and teams on which they played – now you name these postseason veterans.

1.
OF/DH
1973-74 Orioles
1979, 1982 Angels
1986 Red Sox
1987 Twins
1988 A's

2.
OF/IF
1990-91 Pirates
1996 Orioles
1997 Marlins
1999 Mets
2000 Braves

3.
P
1984 Cubs
1988-90, 1992 A's
1996 Cardinals
1998 Red Sox

4.
1B/3B/OF
2007 Red Sox
2008 Rays
2009 Yankees
2010 Braves

5.
P
1981 Expos
1987 Twins
1990 Red Sox
1992 Braves

POSTSEASON VETERANS (2ND INNING ANSWERS)

1. Don Baylor

2. Bobby Bonilla

3. Dennis Eckersley

4. Eric Hinske

5. Jeff Reardon

ROD CAREW ★★★ Played 1967–1985

Rodney Cline Carew, who won seven American League batting titles, compiled a lifetime batting average of .328 and 3,053 hits. He led the league twice in triples, once in runs scored, and three times with most hits in a season (203 in 1973, 218 in 1974 and 239 in 1977). He was inducted into the Baseball Hall of Fame in 1991.

CAREER STATISTICS

Batting average	.328
At bats	9,315
Hits	3,053
Doubles	445
Home runs	92
Runs scored	1,424
Runs batted in	1,015
Bases on balls	1,018

Rod Carew was one of baseball's most proficient "table setters"—he finished his 19 seasons with a career on-base percentage of .393. He got on base at a rate exceeding .400 seven times and exceeded .390 three times. Carew compiled 15 seasons in which his average exceeded .300 and ten seasons in which his strikeouts never rose above 50. His formula for success was to put the ball in play as many times as possible.

This included bunting. Batting left-handed, he developed a superior bunting ability, often beating out a "sacrifice bunt" for a base hit. His bunting ability gave him a huge advantage: infielders had to play close to prevent the bunt. And when they did, he shot the ball by them into the outfield. He honed his bunting skill with practice bunts that he rolled to a stop at various lengths along the foul lines.

After finishing his 12th season with the Minnesota Twins in 1978—in which he won his final American League batting title with a .333 batting average—Carew moved to the California Angels. His presence had an immediate impact as the Angels won the American League Western Division title. They lost the league championship series to the Baltimore Orioles in four games, despite Carew's lofty batting average of .412.

Rod Carew is one of four major league players who were born in the Panama Canal Area. The others are infielder Mike Eden, pitcher Tom Hughes and pitcher Pat Scantlebury, who collectively appeared in a mere 25 major league games vs. 2,469 games played by Carew.

Carew earned hit number 3,000 in 1985. Carew made the All-Star team eighteen consecutive years.

THE HITTERS

WON TITLES AS PLAYER & MANAGER

Success as a Major League Baseball player rarely translates to success as manager. Alan Trammell, Billy Herman, Ted Williams and Cookie Lavagetto are just a few great ballplayers who had poor managerial stints. In contrast, numerous great managers failed as players. Tony La Russa, Sparky Anderson and Bobby Cox all had their cups of coffee. Walter Alston's first major league at-bat for the 1936 Cardinals was his last (he struck out). Anderson got a full-time job at second base with the Phillies in 1959, but hit only .218 and lost his roster spot after the Phils finished 23 games behind Alston's World Champion Dodgers.

Then there's the rare case where an individual is as successful a manager as he was a player. Excluding several player-manager champs, below are examples of men who won World Series titles during their playing days and tasted WS victory again as a manager. Each question refers to a single person, with player titles listed first and manager championships second.

	TEAMS	TITLE YEARS (PLAYER THEN MGR.)
1.	New York Yankees	1996, 1998-99
	New York Yankees	2009
2.	Baltimore Orioles	1966, 1970
	New York Mets	1986
3.	New York Yankees	1977, 1978
	Cincinnati Reds	1990
4.	Cleveland Indians	1948
	New York Yankees	1978
5.	Los Angeles Dodgers	1981, 1988
	Los Angeles Angels of Anaheim	2002
6.	Brooklyn Dodgers	1955
	Los Angeles Dodgers	1959
	New York Mets	1969

	TEAMS	TITLES (PLAYER THEN MGR.)
7.	New York Yankees	1947, 1952
	New York Yankees	1961, 1962
8.	New York Giants	1922
	New York Yankees	1949-53, 1956, 1958
9.	St. Louis Cardinals	1946
	Milwaukee Braves	1957
	St. Louis Cardinals	1967
10.	New York Giants	1954
	Oakland A's	1974
11.	New York Yankees	1951-53, 1956
	New York Yankees	1977
12.	Brooklyn Dodgers - demoted as pitcher during regular season for call-up of Sandy Koufax	1955
	Los Angeles Dodgers	1981, 1988

Won Titles as Player & Manager (answers)

1. Joe Girardi

2. Davey Johnson

3. Lou Piniella

4. Bob Lemon

5. Mike Scioscia

6. Gil Hodges

7. Ralph Houk

8. Casey Stengel

9. Red Schoendienst

10. Al Dark

11. Billy Martin

12. Tommy Lasorda

HONUS WAGNER ★★★ Played 1987–1917

John Peter "Honus" Wagner batted .300 or higher in 16 of his first 17 years as a professional ball player. In the one year that he fell short, he hit .299. Wagner won eight National League batting titles playing shortstop for the Pittsburgh Pirates from 1900 to 1917. He collected 3,418 hits. He was one of the first players inducted into the Baseball Hall of Fame in 1936.

CAREER STATISTICS

Batting average	.327
At bats	10,441
Hits	3,418
Doubles	643
Home runs	101
Runs scored	1,735
Runs batted in	1,732
Bases on balls	963

As baseball legend has it, Honus Wagner was signed as a major leaguer when a scout saw him throwing chunks of coal at a train's coal car. The story is essentially true. The arm was so impressive that Ed Barrow didn't even give Wagner a batting tryout, feeling that anyone who could throw like that must be a complete ball player. Barrow's instincts were correct. In 1897, Wagner's first season, he batted .335 for the Louisville Cardinals, which were then a member of the National League. He was traded to the Pirates on December 8, 1899 with eleven teammates for four Pirates and $25,000.

Wagner excelled for the Pirates as a great fielding shortstop—some say the best ever to play the game—but foremost he was a fearsome hitter. In was an era when total games played were often 10 to 30 games fewer than today's 162-game schedule and runs scored were more frequently produced with a single, stolen base and another single. Wagner at one time or another led the league in every offensive category except home runs, from doubles (including a personal best of 45 in 1900), to triples (personal best of 22 in 1900) to RBI (personal best of 126 in 1901), to runs scored (personal best of 105 in 1902), to stolen bases (personal best of 61 in 1907).

Honus Wagner disliked cigarettes. When he discovered that his baseball card was being packaged with cigarettes, he made them destroy as many cards as possible. Not all were destroyed, however. Thus, baseball card collectors today pay handsome sums for this scarce but valuable trading card.

THE HITTERS

Pitching Greats' Most Frequently Faced

This category involves pitching greats and the one batter they each faced most often in their careers. Considering longevity characteristic to many of these hurlers, it's also reflected by the men who stood in against them. Needless to say, you'll find a number of Hall of Famers on each end of most questions. Items to consider are leagues and divisions in which the pitchers competed. Note: Rather than scorecard at-bats, we're talking career plate appearances here.

1. Greg Maddux – He managed to weather the storm this man brought to the plate, surrendering only 8 home runs to him in 154 meetings. Remarkably, Maddux emerged unscathed as the eye of that storm passed over him. Since 1998, he's only given up 5 hits to this man, none of them homers.

2. Nolan Ryan – The man he faced most often was this great contact-hitting third baseman who, along with 29 hits, only K'd 18 times while standing on the tracks of the Ryan Express.

3. Sandy Koufax – The three men struck out by him the most times are Vada Pinson, Wally Post and this HOF shortstop who also connected for 7 career HRs off Koufax.

4. Jim Palmer – It's logical that Palmer would come across this division rival 197 times in his career. After all, the batter holds the American League record for career at-bats.

5. Bob Gibson – Despite holding him to a .259 average, Gibson served up more HRs (10) and walks (24) to this man than any other person he had the opportunity to intimidate.

6. Tom Seaver – Seaver was most familiar with seeing this HOFer digging in against him. Understandably, he was very conscious of the dangers of allowing this man access to the basepaths.

7. Steve Carlton – They battled each other in the NL East for more than a decade. The hitter did well against the great lefty, hitting .321 lifetime, including .467 as part of his MVP year in 1979.

8. Dennis Eckersley – When the Eck faced him as a starter, this guy was an MVP shortstop. When the Eck faced him as a closer, this guy was an MVP center fielder. Of the eighty-nine times they faced off, at-bat eighty-three was the most memorable. It was September 3, 1991: division races in the stretch, bottom of the ninth, two on, two out, home team down 3-2…walk-off home run!

9. Dave Stewart – The A's three straight division titles from 1988-90 were book-ended by first-place finishes by a division rival. That rival ended up winning the World Series each of those years, thanks in large part to the efforts of a great player Stewart faced 104 times in his mound career.

10. Mariano Rivera – The Red Sox have gotten to Rivera a few times in his attempts to close the door on them. Safe to say, he's more aware of it being ajar every time this man steps to the plate against him, which has been forty-one instances.

PITCHING GREATS' MOST FREQUENTLY FACED (ANSWERS)

1. Barry Bonds

2. George Brett

3. Ernie Banks

4. Carl Yastrzemski

5. Billy Williams

6. Lou Brock

7. Keith Hernandez

8. Robin Yount

9. Kirby Puckett

10. Manny Ramirez

STILL SLUGGING AT 40

Amazingly, only ten men forty years or older have hit at least 20 home runs. Many of them have occurred relatively recently. Of course, a few Hall of Famers exist among these names. Others are well known themselves. Name as many as you can.

1. In 1987, this Tiger, who once claimed an alien spacecraft landed in his backyard, became the only man ever to hit 30 HRs as a forty-year-old.
2. This man's last HR (521) was perhaps his most famous because it came in his last at-bat. He was forty-one when he hit it, one of 29 total home runs in his splendid final season.
3. This forty-year old Giant had not gone completely sour in 1957 when he spanked 26 homers. Can you name this former Cubs MVP?
4. Being drafted in three professional sports signified a great athletic career. While others in the field were winding down their playing days, his 1992 season at age forty was one of his best. He hit 26 HRs with 108 RBI while DH-ing his team to the World Series title, and, thanks to a brand-new retractable roof at his home stadium, kept seagulls out of his way.
5. Getting to 500 career homers necessitated a 20-HR season at age forty for this Hall of Famer. Fittingly, he hit them as a midseason addition to the same team he won Rookie of the Year with in 1977, twenty years prior.
6. This Astro had a solid 2006 by hitting 21 homers at age forty. Although, being the career leader in hit-by-pitches can't help a guy's incontinence.
7. This hugely underrated player holds the record for most career home runs without ever hitting 30 in a year. That mark means a lot of 20-HR seasons (eleven to be exact), one of which came in a great 1999 season that saw him make the All-Star team as a forty-year-old. Who was this White Sox great?
8. He hammered 20 homers at age forty in 1974, the season in which he broke a certain age-old record.
9. As the last man's new batting mark ripened with age, so did this man's swing. He hit 26 and 28 homers at age forty-one and forty-two in 2006 and 2007, respectively, before leaving the game under dubious circumstances.
10. You've probably heard your uncle say it before: "I remember when the pitchers used to hit and there was no such thing as a designated hitter!" In that case, they've been around long enough to see this Mariner develop into the greatest DH in baseball history, a role he fulfilled admirably until the age of forty-one. His second-to-last season in 2003 saw him gangplank twenty-four pitchers for home runs.

STILL SLUGGING AT 40 (ANSWERS)

1. Darrell Evans

2. Ted Williams

3. Hank Sauer

4. Dave Winfield

5. Eddie Murray

6. Craig Biggio

7. Harold Baines

8. Hank Aaron

9. Barry Bonds

10. Edgar Martinez

MISCELLANEOUS MILESTONES (2ND INNING)

More barroom ammunition...

1. Who has won the most World Series rings of any player in baseball history? He's got one for each finger and thumb.

2. Who played the most MLB games without ever having the chance to play in a postseason game? Is telling you he's a Cub a hint or a given?

3. In 1979, this Cardinal became the first player to collect 100 hits from each side of the plate. Who is this temperamental shortstop that was later shipped out of town to San Diego for a young replacement (a kid named Ozzie Smith)?

4. On August 4, 1982, this player had two hits – for two different teams. After a 1 for 2 day game as a Met, he was traded to the Expos in time to tally a pinch-hit against Philadelphia later that night.

5. Who hit the first grand slam in All-Star Game history? It happened in the fiftieth anniversary of the midsummer classic in the place where it all began – Comiskey Park. Dress yourself with decorative bunting if you can name the Giant hurler who surrendered this grand HR.

6. What Cubs fireballer became the first NL pitcher to ring up 20 Ks in a game? It happened in 1998, his rookie season. Unfortunately, arm troubles marred his career soon after.

7. On April 23, 1999, this Cardinal became the only man to tattoo two grand slams in the same inning.

8. In 2004, this pitcher won the deciding games in the Division Series, League Championship Series and World Series – an unprecedented feat.

9. Who is the first player to have at least 30 HRs and 100 RBI in his first ten seasons? His remarkable feat began in 2001.

MISCELLANEOUS MILESTONES (2ND INNING ANSWERS)

1. Yogi Berra

2. Ernie Banks

3. Garry Templeton

4. Joel Youngblood

5. Fred Lynn and Atlee Hammaker

6. Kerry Wood

7. Fernando Tatis

8. Derek Lowe

9. Albert Pujols

GEORGE BRETT ★★★ Played 1973–1993

CAREER STATISTICS

George Howard Brett is fourteenth on the all-time hit list with a total of 3,154 in his 21-year career. He is sixth on the all-time doubles list, with 665. He led the American League in batting average three times, hits three times, triples three times and doubles twice. Brett retired after the 1993 season with a lifetime .305 average and was inducted into the Baseball Hall of Fame in 1999.

Batting average	.305
At bats	10,349
Hits	3,154
Doubles	665
Home runs	317
Runs scored	1,583
Runs batted in	1,595
Bases on balls	1,096

George Brett, legendary batting coach Charley Lau's star pupil, averaged over .300 in eleven of his twenty-one years. He also had 14 years of double-digit home runs, although he never thought of himself as a power hitter. Twice he compiled more than 200 hits in a season, and four times he knocked in more than 100 runs.

Brett had 212 hits in 1979 to lead the league, but his shining season came in 1980. In September of that year, he was batting .393. Many thought that Brett would break the .400 mark, a feat that hadn't been done since Ted Williams hit .406 in 1941. During his run at .400 opposing pitchers were uncertain of what pitch to throw to Brett. He could hit almost any pitch in any location: high, low, inside, or outside. And it didn't matter what type of pitch was thrown: fastball, cutter, sinker, curve ball, slider or a change-up. When asked what type of pitch he liked to look for, Brett said, "I just look for the ball." Brett needed a hot streak—a hit in every two at bats—over the final eleven games to cross the coveted .400 mark. Unfortunately, he didn't make it. But he posted a spectacular .390 average.

Injuries played a role in Brett's career—they periodically kept him out of the lineup throughout his career. Brett had only six seasons in which he played more than 150 games. The unforgiving Astroturf that covered the field of the Kansas City Royals contributed to the litany of injuries that did harm over the

George Brett is the only player in major league history to win a batting title in three different decades. He led all American League batters in 1976, 1980 and 1990.

years to Brett's shoulder, wrist, hands, back, ribs, knees, ankles and feet and kept Brett from compiling even greater hitting statistics.

THE HITTERS

DYNAMIC DUOS

Each query below asks you to name a pair of ballplayers who the trivia gods have linked together in some fashion or another.

1. Name the only co-MVP Award winners in major league history. These two Senior Circuit stars shared the accolade in 1979.

2. 1975 was a special year for the Boston Red Sox, aided in great part by a pair of stellar rookies dubbed the "Gold Dust Twins." One became the first rookie MVP in history. The other – whose regular-season injury denied the Sox a powerful postseason bat – won league MVP three seasons later.

3. They finished one-two in the NL's Cy Young voting, but were given equal share of the World Series MVP Award after leading their team to a thrilling 4-3 Series victory in 2001. Name this brilliant lefty-righty duo.

4. What two Seattle Mariners each won ten Gold Gloves navigating the outfield?

5. In 1958, the San Francisco Giants fielded a Rookie of the Year at first base who would go on to win an NL MVP Award and be voted to the Hall of Fame. In 1959, the San Francisco Giants fielded a Rookie of Year at first base who would go on to win an NL MVP Award and be voted to the Hall of Fame. Name both of these great sluggers.

6. For much of the twentieth century, Philadelphia baseball was divided into National and American League "fiefdoms," but in 1933 a pair of tyrannical sluggocrats united the Philly duchies under a common "Triple Crown." Wielding splintered wooden scepters, each of these Broad Street Marquis conquered their league in batting, home runs and RBI. Can you name this pair of sluggers?

7. The 1970s Big Red Machine was lubricated by a stellar double play combo who paired for four straight Gold Gloves from 1974-77. Can you name this slick 6-4 combo?

8. In 1951, two catchers won their league MVP Award. They were the only double backstops awarded their circuit's top performer in the same year. They paired up again as league MVPs in 1955. Name them both.

9. In 1968, two pitchers won Most Valuable Player honors in their respective leagues – unquestionably aided by favorable alterations to mound dimensions.

10. The 1948 Boston Braves won the NL pennant with a solid four-man pitching rotation, but two of the hurlers were instrumental in clinching the title during the season's final weeks. Starting with a crucial Labor Day doubleheader, the alliterative pair posted an amazing 8-0 record in a twelve-game span – inspiring a lyrical tribute by Beantown sports writer Gerald Hern. While Hern effectively omitted the names Bill Voiselle and Vern Bickford from history, we've only omitted the names of the other two Braves starters from the poem's rhyme scheme:

> First we'll use _____,
> Then we'll use _____
> Then an off day
> Followed by rain
> Back will come ____
> Followed by ____
> And followed , we hope
> By two days of rain

DYNAMIC DUOS (ANSWERS)

1. Keith Hernandez and Willie Stargell

2. Fred Lynn and Jim Rice

3. Randy Johnson and Curt Schilling

4. Ken Griffey Jr. and Ichiro Suzuki

5. Orlando Cepeda and Willie McCovey

6. Chuck Klein (Phillies) and Jimmie Foxx (A's)

7. Joe Morgan (2B) and Dave Concepcion (SS)

8. Roy Campanella (NL) and Yogi Berra (AL)

9. Bob Gibson (NL) and Denny McLain (AL)

10. Warren Spahn and Johnny Sain

Battery Mates (2nd Inning)

Another pile of catchers to sort through as you identify the pitchers who threw to them over the course of exceptional careers. GC refers to the number of games each catcher caught for their battery mate of note.

	CATCHER	GC		CATCHER	GC
1.	Todd Hundley	54	2.	Gregg Zaun	75
	Jim Sundberg	45		Carlos Ruiz	56
	Jamie Quirk	42		Darrin Fletcher	52
	Jason Varitek	33		Rod Barajas	50

3.	Del Crandall	318	4.	Rick Dempsey	158
	Phil Masi	68		Elrod Hendricks	101
	Joe Torre	63		Andy Etchebarren	98

5.	Jim Hegan	241	6.	Harry Danning	130
	Rollie Hemsley	115		Gus Mancuso	125
	Frankie Pytlak	32		Shanty Hogan	101

7.	Joe Mauer	79	8.	Terry Steinbach	164
	A.J. Pierzynski	71		Steve Yeager	64
	Henry Blanco	37		Mike Scioscia	54
	Mike Redmond	28		Mickey Tettleton	44
	Brian Schneider	25		Pat Borders	43

9.	Bruce Benedict	148	10.	Ossee Schreckengost	198
	Biff Pocoroba	98		Tubby Spencer	23
	Joe Torre	86		Tacks Latimer	6
	Dale Murphy	23		Pop Schriver	3
	Bob Uecker	21		Farmer Steelman	2
				Bert Blue	1
				Jiggs Donahue	1

BATTERY MATES (2ND INNING ANSWERS)

Pitcher	Career Starts
1. Bret Saberhagen	371
2. Roy Halladay	352
3. Warren Spahn	665
4. Jim Palmer	521
5. Bob Feller	484
6. Carl Hubbell	433
7. Johan Santana	263
8. Dave Stewart	348
9. Phil Niekro	716
10. Rube Waddell	340

MEL OTT ★★★ Played 1926–1947

Mel Thomas Ott was a power-hitting outfielder for the New York Giants for 22 years, spanning 1926 to 1947. Ott, who is twenty-third on the all-time home run list with 511, led the National League for six seasons in home runs, RBIs and bases on balls. Ott was inducted into the Baseball Hall of Fame in 1951.

CAREER STATISTICS

Batting average	.304
At bats	9,456
Hits	2,876
Doubles	488
Home runs	511
Runs scored	1,859
Runs batted in	1,860
Bases on balls	1,708

Melvin "Mel" Thomas Ott debuted with the New York Giants in the major leagues on April 27, 1926, at the tender age of seventeen. He spent his entire career with the Giants. Despite playing very little in his first few years, Ott blossomed in his third year when he batted .322 with 18 home runs, 26 doubles, 4 triples and 77 RBI in a mere 124 games.

Over the next fourteen years he became a model of consistency, averaging 148 games per season and powering the Giants' attack with double-digit season averages of 30 round trippers, 29 doubles and 98 RBI. In the first inning of Game 1 of the 1933 World Series, Ott blasted a two-run home run into the right field stands of the Polo Grounds. Then in the tenth inning of the final game, with the score tied 3-3, Ott smacked another home run, giving the Giants the World Series championship over the Washington Senators.

Ott became the first National League player to hit more than 500 home runs. Ironically, in 1929, when Ott compiled his highest home run total, 42, rival Chuck Klein of the Philadelphia Phillies hit 43, thus edging out Ott for the home run crown. Ott was known for his high front leg kick as he prepared to stride—the first acknowledged power hitter to employ this technique.

Although often in the running for the National League MVP–Ott was on the ballot in thirteen seasons, finishing as high as third, fourth, fifth, sixth and seventh in different voting years—the twelve-time All Star never gained this honor.

THE SLUGGERS

MIDSEASON SWITCH

In each of the following cases, one or more players changed team affiliations during the regular season and, while doing so, precipitated a trivial anecdote worthy of note.

1. A boorish disposition and bestial batting approach kept this "home-run-or-nothing" behemoth from finding stability in major league clubhouses during his sixteen-year career. Never was he more itinerant than during the 1977 season, a year in which he played for a record four different teams in four separate divisions. He also took advantage of the opportunity, as he set records by homering with all four clubs, which included the distinction of being the only human to do so as a Yankee and Met in the same season.

2. By the time this ballplayer was traded back to his hometown team in June 1989, he was a thirty-year old multi-millionaire and certified sports celebrity – and the small-market team of inexperienced youngsters he left five years prior was now a 100-win juggernaut and reigning pennant winner. As talented as they were, their midseason acquisition provided the missing piece to securing a World Series title. Four years later, the same player would be traded midseason to a new team and reprise his role as a galvanizing force toward another World Championship.

3. Speaking of truant league leading in major statistical categories, this skinny Cardinals All-Star was sent waddling westward to play out the season with the Oakland A's in 1990. He lost out on a World Series ring, but found his .335 batting average right where he left it – atop the National League with enough at-bats to qualify as official Senior Circuit batting champion.

4. In 1983, this sweet Texas lefty had his All-Star season cut in two when he was traded to the Dodgers in August. He went 2-3 in Los Angeles, allowing almost six runs per game, but finished the season as the American League leader in ERA. His 2.42 ERA average in 174 innings was enough to qualify for best in his former circuit. Who was this absentee title winner?

5. Who is the only player to hit 20 home runs for two teams in the same season?

6. Perhaps the greatest turnaround by a player traded midseason occurred in 1984, when an ineffectual Cleveland pitcher scrapped a 4-5 start to start fresh in the NL as a Cub. No one could have imagined that the resurrected hurler would go 16-1 in the next three months, win the Cy Young and lead the ill-fated Cubs to their first playoff appearance in forty years. No one.

7. In an effort to shore up their bullpen for a late-season playoff run, the Red Sox swung and missed in this infamous 1990 trade for Houston reliever Larry Andersen. Andersen pitched well in the final month, but took the first loss in Oakland's ALCS sweep of Boston. The price for his month and a half of service was a top AAA prospect from Pawtucket who would immediately win NL Rookie of the Year in 1991, league MVP in '94 and retire as the greatest slugger in Astros history and a likely Hall of Fame inductee.

8. The sting of Boston's front-office gaffe in 1990 – along with eighty-six years of turmoil – was assuaged by a more fortuitous deal fourteen years later. As part of a four-team trade in 2004, the Red Sox parted ways with a coulda-been franchise legend in exchange for a slick-fielding replacement from Montreal and a sly first-sacker from Minnesota. Both would play important roles in Boston's eventual World Series win. Name the player the Red Sox traded away and, for extra points, the two players Boston received in return.

MIDSEASON SWITCH (ANSWERS)

1. Dave Kingman

2. Rickey Henderson

3. Willie McGee

4. Rick Honeycutt

5. Mark McGwire

6. Rick Sutcliffe

7. Jeff Bagwell

8. Nomar Garciaparra/Orlando Cabrera and Doug Mientkiewicz

100 WINS WITH TWO FRANCHISES

This category tells the tale of pitchers whose greatness must be told in two volumes. Each managed to amass at least 100 wins with one team in the first half of their career, then switch teams and total another 100 for a different franchise. Name these greats by their career splits. Note: The pitcher's overall wins and losses, which may have come from teams and years not listed, appear in the gray-shaded boxes.

1.

Years	W	L
1991-2008	270	153
Orioles (10 yrs)	147	81
Yankees (8 yrs)	123	72

2.

Years	W	L
1976-98	245	193
Orioles (11 yrs)	108	93
Expos (8 yrs)	100	72

3.

	W	L
1986-2008	355	227
Braves (11 yrs)	194	88
Cubs (10 yrs)	133	112

4.

	W	L
1890-1911	511	316
Indians (9 yrs)	241	135
Red Sox (8 yrs)	192	112

5.

	W	L
1925-41	300	141
Philly A's (9 yrs)	195	79
Red Sox (8 yrs)	105	62

6.

	W	L
1911-30	373	208
Cubs (9 yrs)	128	83
Phillies (8 yrs)	190	91

7.

	W	L
1966-93	324	292
Astros (9 yrs)	106	94
Angels (8 yrs)	138	121

100 WINS WITH TWO FRANCHISES (ANSWERS)

1. Mike Mussina

2. Dennis Martinez

3. Greg Maddux

4. Cy Young

5. Lefty Grove

6. Pete Alexander

7. Nolan Ryan

BASEBALL LINEAGES: PITTSBURGH PIRATES SHORTSTOPS

PITTSBURGH PIRATES SHORTSTOPS			
YEARS	**SS**	**YEARS**	**SS**
1901	Bones Ely	1963	Dick Schofield
		1964-73	**5.?**
1902-16	**1.?**	1969	Freddie Patek
		1974-78	Frank Taveras
1917-20	3 players		
1921-24	**2.?**	1979-81	**6.?**
1925-28	Glenn Wright	1982-84	**7.?**
		1985	Sammy Khalifa
1929-30	Dick Bartell	1986-88	Rafael Belliard
1931	Tommy Thevenow		
1932-41	**3.?**	1989-96	**8.?**
		1997-2000	4 players
1942-54	8 players	2001-09	**9.?**
1955-62	**4.?**	2010-11	Ronny Cedeno

BASEBALL LINEAGES: PITTSBURGH PIRATES SHORTSTOPS (ANSWERS)

1. Honus Wagner

2. Rabbit Maranville

3. Arky Vaughan

4. Dick Groat

5. Gene Alley

6. Tim Foli

7. Dale Berra

8. Jay Bell

9. Jack Wilson

ENDED CAREER WITH THIS TEAM (BOTTOM OF THE NINTH...

One on, two outs, 5-all tie. It's up to you to come through and push across a run in this deadlocked trivia contest. If not, we can always play extra innings.

1. Ty Cobb

2. Hank Greenberg

3. Reggie Jackson

4. Ralph Kiner

5. Ted Kluszewski

6. Mickey Lolich

7. Roger Maris

8. Christy Mathewson

9. Ron Santo

10. Duke Snider

11. Billy Williams

12. Curt Flood

ENDED CAREER WITH THIS TEAM (BOTTOM OF THE NINTH ANSWERS)

1. Philadelphia A's (1928)

2. Pittsburgh Pirates (1947)

3. Oakland A's (1987)

4. Cleveland Indians (1955)

5. Los Angeles Angels (1961)

6. San Diego Padres (1979)

7. St. Louis Cardinals (1968)

8. Cincinnati Reds (1916)

9. Chicago White Sox (1974)

10. San Francisco Giants (1964)

11. Oakland A's (1976)

12. Washington Senators (1971)

To be continued ...